Carolynn,

Enjoy the book!

M.

Author Mile

# ARM CANDY

## *A Celebrity Escort's Tales from the Red Carpet*

By
Christopher Gaida

With
Michael Aloisi

ISBN: 978-0-9884468-1-6
Library of Congress Control Number: 2012954731

Cover Credits:
Cover Photo Shoot Produced by Vincent De Paul
Photography by: Bradford Rogne - www.bradfordrogne.com
Models: Courtney Guarino and Lorraine Provencio
Tuxedo by: Angelo Rossi at Hollywood Suit Outlet
Graphic Design by: Kevin Hill
Special thanks to Tommy Hilfiger

First Published by *AuthorMike Ink*, 1/31/2013

www.AuthorMikeInk.com

*AuthorMike Ink* and its logos are trademarked by *AuthorMike Ink*.

**Printed in the United States of America**

This book is dedicated to my loving grandmothers who have always inspired me to go after my dreams and taught me to fight for what I believe in.

Catherine Heim          Helen Gaida

This book is also in memory of Oliver Gaida. Oliver meant the world to me and was always there happily waiting as I came home from these experiences. In March 2012, he died from Cancer after bravely battling it for over nine months.

# TABLE OF CONTENTS

# INTRODUCTION:
# IN THE BEGINNING... THERE WERE STARS!

## Hollywood, CA

My fingers intertwined hers. My heart raced. My palms sweat. Nervously, I looked at her giant, toothy smile. Was this real? As I stared at a face I'd seen dozens of times on the big screen, the world seemed to stop. There was no noise. I felt nothing. I just saw her glowing as she kept the smile that compelled millions to fall in love with her. A bright flash struck my eyes. I blinked. This *was* real. I was holding the hand of one of the biggest movie stars in the history of film...Julia Roberts.

Moments earlier, hundreds of cameras flashed their bright bulbs and photographers screamed Julia's name in hopes of one good photo. Yet, here I was holding hands and talking with her as if we were best friends since high school. I've come a long way from small town Pennsylvania. Thinking back, it feels like a lifetime ago since the first time I watched Hollywood's finest play dress-up in "The Land of Make Believe".

I'm not mentioned in tabloids or paid million dollar contracts for movie roles, yet I still rub elbows with Hollywood elite. I experience the glitz of award shows and the glam of after parties. And while you don't know my name, you've actually seen me on television or in photos without even realizing it. It's okay; you were probably too busy looking at Julia, Angelina, Sandra, Jennifer, Mariah, Paris, etc., to notice the handsome gentlemen walking with her. You've probably flipped through *US Weekly* or one of the many other star stalker magazines to look at the post-*Golden Globes* coverage and seen my smiling face behind someone wealthier and well known. More often than not, it's only my arm or a sliver of my smiling face in the shot. The rest of me is tragically cropped out by an overzealous editor who doesn't want a 'nobody' taking up valuable page space. Regardless, I was there, experiencing everything in awe.

I'll write more about Julia and my unforgettable encounters with her later, but before you get too deep into this book, you need to know these are *my* stories. It is about *my* life working behind-the-scenes of entertainment award shows. No one has ever written what it is like for an average person to access this A-list lifestyle. While I won't hold back writing what I've seen and experienced, this book was not written to create a scandal. It is to raise awareness of a life most never realized existed and to show a look behind-the-scenes from an everyday person's prospective. I am betting most never Celebrity Escorts existed, because it's been kept a secret for over 30 years.

Well, now I'm ready to share my adventures about my *non-sexual* career as a celebrity escort, as well as many other Hollywood secrets. And let's just say some people are not happy about it!

My name is Christopher Gaida and I have escorted many of the world's biggest and brightest stars for over twelve years. What I had anticipated as a "one night stand," became a career that defines a great part of me. It opened my mind and also doors to life's possibilities. It has led me from The Big Apple to The Big Avocado, known as Los

Angeles. It's not always pretty, but it is fascinating, hilarious and full of behind-the-scenes stories even *TMZ* isn't privy to.

Now sit back, pour a glass of champagne or sparkling cider, and learn about this secret world people rarely speak about. There are bitches, surprises, and even a kangaroo! Let me tell how I went from blue collar to black tie--how my American dream has come true. My wish is to inspire you to go for your dreams, no matter how far reaching they seem. I hope you enjoy this biography from someone who was neither born with a silver spoon in my mouth or to a family already in the industry. I, too, was once star struck and hoped to just meet a celebrity once. I never thought I would have the privilege of spending over a decade with hundreds of them.

Welcome to the Secret World of a celebrity escort....

# THE HOLLYWOOD CELEBRITY ESCORT

The first thing most people associate with the word "escort" is high-class prostitution. If you are one of those people, don't worry. I thought the same thing when I first heard about the job. Sadly, the word has been sullied over time. When people ask me about my career, I always follow up "escort" with, "not that kind". This is most difficult when I run into my parent's friends at a Pennsylvania grocery store or worse yet, church! I make these moments enjoyable by pausing a few extra seconds before explaining what the job really entails. Their expressions are usually priceless!

Regardless of the connotations it may evoke, a Celebrity Escort is a professional, exciting and exclusive non-sexual job that handles some of the world's most famous people. In my opinion, escorting is a necessity to make award shows function properly. Producers are busy with the big picture, so we are brought in to handle the smaller details and logistics. It's also a personalized touch to have special attention given to a presenting, nominated or performing celebrity.

As an escort, my job is to accompany celebrities to award shows, benefits, and parties. We are required to be next to our assigned celebrity at all times. We must never be seen without them. Also, we act as an added buffer between the celebrity and other crew, fans and general public. If they have security with them already, we work closely with their team to provide with the best possible service. Celebrity Escorts are both male and female. Even as a male celebrity escort, I can

1

be paired with another male. As I mentioned before, it is not a sexual thing. Some celebrities do prefer to have the opposite sex accompany them, but mostly they want someone who is exceptional and professional.

Some people think my job is to make a celebrity look good. However, most of them are already hot, talented, charming people, and have been for years without me. Other people have accused me of being a star f*ucker, attention seeker or virtually useless. This is certainly not true either. My job has two very important functions.

1) First, I remove celebrities' fears and distractions so they can be themselves. Having a celebrity escort is like wearing a pair of shoes - a perfect fit is priceless, a bad fit could mean a trip and fall. Many shows are live and things change rather quickly. Celebrities need someone to stay on top of everything and communicate any last minute changes or issues. An inattentive escort may not get the talent backstage in time or cause them to miss out on benefits such as the gift lounge. With a good escort, the night flows flawlessly because the celebrity is never aware of prevented or extinguished fires.

2) The second main function is to support the producers. There are so many moving elements when it comes to an award show production. Having a celebrity escort helps maintain control and communicate possible issues. Escorts help smooth things over if a situation arises that a celebrity is unhappy about. I have been in this situation many times and have even been called the Celebrity Whisperer because I have always been able to diffuse a problem and calm a situation. Escorts need

to make both celebrities and the producer's happy, which can sometimes be difficult, especially if they want conflicting things.

## A Typical Show

There are a small group of us that typically work many different shows and an even smaller few, such as myself, that have worked just about every award show there is at least once. If a celebrity or their publicist doesn't ask for a specific escort, one will be provided for them. Many celebrities don't realize they can (and in my opinion *absolutely* should) request a specific escort just as they would a make-up artist. Having someone they are familiar with is always better than a random assignment--their skill set and personality unknown. I think it's like playing Russian roulette and there are many dangers that could come from this.

**When I am escorting, I am able to meet celebrities other than the celebrity I am working with. Here I am with David Beckham by the press tents at the *2010 Teen Choice Awards.***

Many of the best publicists do request specific escorts because their job will be made easier, too. Luckily, I have been specifically requested or hired many times. I enjoy developing these long-term relationships with such talented people. This only makes me want to work harder for them. All of this is arranged in advance and escorts are told at least one day before the event which celebrity they will be working with.

Once show day has arrived, I typically wait at the top of the red carpet for the star's limo to pull up. This can be very exciting or very boring, as some celebrities arrive later than anticipated. When they do arrive, I greet them, introduce myself (if we haven't already met) and guide them down the red carpet. I make sure they are at ease and provide any interviews the award show producer set up for them or ones they would like to do. This sometimes requires me to guard the train of a celebrity's long dress as people bustle down the carpet. I, myself, have accidentally stepped on a few trains while trying to navigate my talent (sorry Julia Louis-Dreyfus)! Often times there is so much going on it is difficult to get your talent the best exposure possible while also staying out of other people's way. Some celebrities have a road map of the media outlets they will and will not do interviews with. It can be a maze running back and forth while keeping this all straight, especially having to ignore an eager reporter who wants the interview even though the celebrity doesn't. One mistake by me could make an awkward moment on camera and an unhappy celebrity.

On the flip side, I want to make sure the celebrity gets as much press as they would like because this is their moment to shine. I do have to keep in mind timing; if we spend too much time with one reporter, then they will miss coverage at other outlets. Sometimes I have the star's publicist making these decisions, but often I'm on my own. Either way, these are the moments when my Facebook page and cell phone blow up because while news coverage is capturing the celebrity, sometimes there's my mug in the background. My friends and family are always excited. Everyone wants me to take their call so they can see me talking to them live on television. While I do have to admit it's fun knowing I am seen by millions of people, I ignore my calls until my job is done. If I lost focus it would not be fair to the show or the star. However, I will admit I'm guilty of scouring through news coverage the next day searching for my big public appearance and hoping it's not three seconds of me looking stupid.

At this point in the evening, my most important task is to make sure the talent is where the producer's need them the moment the show begins. I may take them to their seat, backstage, dressing room or green room depending on their specific scheduled appearance on the show.

Once the show has begun, producers/director try to make sure the schedule is followed as closely as possible. However, I must know exactly where my celebrity is at all times because timing is crucial and schedules can change at any point. About ten minutes prior to the time they are scheduled to appear on stage, I will bring my star to a stage manager who explains any last minute details. One of the worst things that could happen is losing track of a celebrity moments before needed on stage or having them detained in the rest room. I think we have all watched an award show when someone's name is announced and they do not appear for several seconds. Those seconds seem to last forever causing the show to feel unprofessional. I have made sure this has never occurred during my watch! If a celebrity needs to pee mere minutes before going on stage, I tell them to hold it. It happens more often than you would think and only once has this caused someone to nearly pee his pants. Luckily, I led him running to the rest room with his penis in his hands. I held the bathroom door open as he raced through reaching the urinal just barely in time. Luckily, I was not shot down.

**Olivia Wilde at the *2010 Golden Globes* After Party**
**I'm Tired and a Little Drunk**

Once done with all of their on camera duties for the evening, then they are free to choose where they would like to go next. It could be the gift lounge, press room, dressing room, green room, back to their seat or to their cars if they are planning on sneaking out early. Sometimes they do leave early because of other events they need to attend or because they want to get home. If they have more show duties or are nominated for an award that has not be given out yet, than I am usually directed by the Stage Managers on how much time we have and where they need to be.

Uggie, the dog star from *The Artist* and I sharing stories about our book writing on the 2011 Golden Globes' Red Carpet

At the end of each show, if my talent has not left, I will bring them either to their car, to any remaining press interviews or to an after party. The after party always gets my vote and I will cover this in great detail toward the end of the book.

## Twelve Key Qualities and Responsibilities Required to be a Good Celebrity Escort

So what is required to do the job? I have listed twelve key qualities below. If you are ever asked to do the job you should know there is a lot more than just standing there and looking pretty.

1) Know the full run down of the show.
2) Always be two steps ahead.
3) Know when to stay close and when to keep a distance with your celebrity.
4) Be able to initiate small talk when first meeting your talent. Then quickly know what you should or shouldn't say to specific talent.
5) Know how to read body language, which includes knowing when to pull talent away from fans, and when to leave them alone.
6) Be on time at every point throughout the day.
7) Know various crewmembers and their responsibilities. If your talent has a specific request, then you will know immediately which person to speak with.
8) Be aware of last minute changes. This means even if they are not being told to you directly. You must listen to what is going

on around you to sometimes get that information. Unfortunately, just because you have not been told important information does not mean you are not responsible for not knowing it.

9) Do not be passive! Take charge of a situation immediately.

10) Have a car ready for the star when they want to leave.

11) Be flexible and make the impossible happen.

12) Always be honest! If you don't know the answers to a question say so, but find out immediately.

While being an escort may not be a lifelong career, it's one that is amazing, eye opening, and part of the inner circle fans can only imagine. We get to work with the A-list celebrities on a weekly basis, sit with them in limos, talk to them in green rooms and even become friends with many. It's the only job I know of where you can be a regular Joe one day, then the next day be eating caviar with Tom Hanks, and the following day be walking down the street, with no one ever having a clue you were at the *Oscars*. It's an amazing job, which I am happy to share, so now let's get to it already!

# TWENTY-TWO INSIDER TERMS
# YOU SHOULD KNOW

\

When learning anything new, whether it is karate, cooking or nuclear physics, there is always a vocabulary one should be aware. This is also the case with celebrity escorting and award shows. There are MANY terms used by people who work behind-the-scenes and although it may not be as complicated as engineering, I think it would be interesting for you to understand a few of them upfront. As you read further in the book, some things will be explained, but at least here you will learn some of the basics now if you don't already know them.

If you are the type of person who becomes bored with definitions, then feel free to skip this chapter and when an unfamiliar term comes up, check back here. However, if you are someone who wants to know everything about entertainment and be hip to the lingo, keep reading! You will be privy to some extra information the general public may not know; and when watching an award show on TV, you will have a clear understanding on what is taking place behind-the-scenes.

Some of these terms are simple and you might have heard of them. Others can be confusing at first. But all of them are important and used often in my world. There's only so much storytelling I can tell in a glossary chapter, but hold on tight because once I have this all cleared up, I promise you some interesting experiences.

## 1) Venue

This is the physical place the event is located at. For example, *The Primetime Emmy Awards* happened at the Nokia Theatre in downtown Los Angeles. You would refer to the Nokia Theatre as the venue. What is the venue you're going to be at? I will be at the Nokia Theatre. A very easy term, but if you were asked and didn't know what the person was talking about, they would know you were a rookie. Obviously there is a venue for every award show.

**From the Front Row of the Nokia Theatre
at the *2010 Primetime Emmys*
Minutes Before Everyone Arrived**

## 2) Talent

Talent is the word we use many times when talking about any celebrity. This term is used every day. I never even thought about possible confusion until after I used it with my niece Brittany.

Basically it means "celebrity" or "star" and we use the words interchangeable. If someone asks, "What talent are you with tonight?" I would answer, "I am with Julia Roberts". In this book, I will use this word a lot. In fact, many times people refer to Celebrity Escorts as Talent Escorts. Talent can be a singer, actor or anyone who is going to appear on camera for that event. Please note: talent does not refer to my thoughts about their abilities.

## 3) Walkies

Many people know a Walkie Talkie is a battery-operated radio people use to communicate. We (production people) refer to them just as Walkies. Each one has numerous channels where different people with different functions can communicate separately. For example, celebrity escorts may be on channel 1, dressing room people on channel 2, lighting people on channel 3 and security on channel 4, etc. It would be very annoying to hear other people talking about their functions all-day and hard to get airtime when everyone else is speaking at the same time. With these walkies we can change the channels easily therefore, allowing us to speak to anyone in production at any point. Mostly though, we stay on our assigned channel.

When one person wants to have a long conversation with another on the walkie, they will ask the other person to go to what is called an "open" channel. This is a channel that has not been assigned to anyone at all. These channels are not secured so anyone can go on any channel at any point. If a confidential conversation needs to occur, it is best kept to a face-to-face meeting. Some shows have a limited amount of walkies, so many times only escorts with key talent get them. Most escorts love to get the walkie because it makes them feel important. I have always tried to avoid getting a walkie no matter who I escort because I don't like hearing the crew talking back and forth all night long in my ear. I also hate the headsets they come with because they mess up my spiky hair.

**Walkie Checkout Area at a Typical Show**

In the later years, I bought my own secret service type earpiece so it would fit nicely in my ear and the cord would be hidden under my clothing. I still had to hear all the chatter, but the walkies were always being forced on me anyway, so it was a good compromise.

## 4) Walkie Check

Once a person gets the radio, plugs in the headphones and turns it on, the first thing they do is called a Walkie Check. The term means the person is checking to make sure they are being heard and can hear properly. They would say, "Walkie check" and another person on the same channel would respond, "Good check".

Many times, if the person is not heard it's because the headset was not plugged in properly or the battery on the walkie is low. In order to talk on these walkies, a person pushes a button is located on the side; sometimes you can also find a button on the cord of the headset. They hold the button in while speaking and release it when finished. If no one responds, let's hope it is one of these issues and not because people don't like you!

## 5) Keyed

Occasionally, the button on the walkie may become stuck or the headset was not plugged in correctly and the mic is now "open" allowing everyone on that channel to hear everything the person is saying. This is called being Keyed. Other people on that channel will say something such as "Who is keyed? Can everyone check their walkie to see if they're keyed?" People then should turn off their walkies, make sure the plug on the headset is plugged in properly, and turn on the radio again. If their battery is low, then they need to replace it with a fully charged one.

In addition to being annoying, it could also be dangerous and embarrassing if the person being keyed is unaware of it. If your mic is open then everyone can hear what you and anyone around you is saying. You may be spilling some gossip, but now everyone on that channel will know it and know it was coming from you. Worse yet, if you're keyed and in the rest room....

Yes, being keyed happens often. And frequently the person being keyed is completely unaware. During one award show, an escort was actually trash talking the person who hired her. It was broadcast for everyone to hear, including her boss. Needless to say, that person was fired immediately. When I gossip (don't act like you wouldn't), I make sure the mic is either away from my mouth or the radio is completely off. I can be very honest and bold with my statements, but not all of them should be heard by the people on my channel.

### 6) What's Your Twenty?

"What's your twenty?" is a phrase often heard on the walkies. It means--what is your location or where are you located? The person should then respond with their exact location. Saying you're backstage is not enough. You should give a quick detailed description of your location. Nothing is more frustrating than having to go back and forth on the walkie to get accurate information. Many of these shows are live and any delay makes everyone's job more difficult. A better response would be, "I am backstage left standing next to Katy Perry".

## 7) House

This term means the inside seating area of the venue. The stage is along the front and the house is the entire open room. If there are balconies, then they are referred to as balconies, but all other audience seating is in the house. For example, when you sit and watch a movie in a movie theatre, you are sitting in the house. The lobby is not considered the house.

## 8) Craft Service

Every crewmember and actor usually gets an actual meal break after six hours of working. Meals are usually provided on location at the venue. These are full meals and can be simple or extravagant with items such as steak and seafood. This is not however, craft services.

Craft service is a term widely used on just about every production whether it is film or television, and is most people's favorite term. Basically, it's food provided by the production for the talent and crew. It is not the main meals, but snacks set up for the entire time of shooting.

Whether you're an assistant, a producer, or anyone in between, anything on that table is yours for the taking. Some tables are extra special with fresh fruit cut up, vitamins, aspirin, etc., but all tables have snacks such as chips, yogurt, soda, water, and candy. Craft service is an added benefit everyone enjoys, but sometimes the table can be a curse, as well. Do you know how hard it is to walk by stacks of your favorite candy and food all day long and not eat it?

## 9) Show Rundown

The Show Rundown is a written document that contains a detailed order of the show broken down into individual items. This multi-page document is handed out days before the show taping and is revised numerous times up until moments before the show begins. It is given to most crewmembers so there is a clear communication of what will happen, at what times and in what order. With every new show rundown, they are printed on different colored paper so it is not to confuse anyone with what is the latest document. Each show rundown also contains the date and time it was revised and printed. You can usually find a stack of the latest one on the production office table.

## 10) Call Times

Call Times are the times cast and crew are supposed to report to work and are listed on the Call Sheet. It's just like the time you are expected to show up at work every day. If you are asked to go to work at eight AM, your call time is eight AM. On productions, these times change daily. They are determined for the next day halfway through the current day because producers need to see how far they get before determining the need to return the next day. Production coordinators are usually the people who create the schedule and distribute the call sheets. Everyone who works on set gets a call time including escorts.

## 11) Talent Team

This is the team handling celebrity's logistics during the show. It usually consists of five groups.

A) Talent Bookers–those who negotiate with the celebrities to appear on the show weeks or days before the event.

B) Talent Producers–those who hire the talent bookers and use their connections to make sure celebrities have agreed to come to the event and are happy with the negotiated details.

C) Talent Flow Team–the members who make sure celebrities are in their proper seats and are scheduled on time by either themselves, the escorts, or stage managers. There may be up to ten per show.

D) Escort Manager (also have other titles such as Director)– those who hire the escorts and coordinate all of the celebrities planned movements. They also assign the celebrities to specific escorts and lead the meetings.

E) Talent (Celebrity) Escorts

If effective, the team can create a great experience for all celebrities and help show producers/directors with their vision. I have worked as an escort, part of the talent flow team, and as an escort manager on award shows. I typically enjoy escorting the most because I have the one on one contact with a celebrity for the entire event. Working on the talent flow team is fun and you work with just about all the celebrities for the entire show. However, you don't make the personal connections you do as an escort.

## 12) Prompter or Teleprompter

This is the device talent uses to read their lines while on stage. There is typically also one backstage for them to rehearse with before they come out on stage. Usually, before the show most celebrities will take 5-10 minutes to read through their lines to help familiarize themselves with the material. If they came to rehearsal earlier in the day or the day before, they would have practiced this on stage and looked out at a giant monitor in the center of the house making sure they can see it properly. Some celebrities need a larger font so they won't have to use their glasses. All of this can be figured out if they rehearse in advance. I have seen some celebrities need the font so large it seems as if they were going blind!

The teleprompter is provided so actors don't have to memorize anything. It's also there to help create a more natural appearance when they are speaking. Many times now, the prompter is a glass screen placed directly in front of the lens of a camera or to the immediate side. There are many types of prompters. But they all do the same thing: feed the lines to whoever is presenting. They allow the actor to look into the camera while reading. If done properly, you can't tell they are reading anything at all. News reporters and even the president use prompters when giving speeches.

## 13) Live to Tape

The term "live" is pretty simple; it means you are watching it as it actually happens. Those viewers at home usually have a seven second delay. I don't know of any show that would not have a few seconds delay, but it is as close to live as can be. Shows can be tricky with this and I will explain further when I list out a few award show secrets. "Live to tape", on the other hand, means they film it as if the show was live, but it will air at a later date or time. While they do have the luxury to stop the show to film something over, typically they try not to. This gives the viewers the feeling of it being live even when it isn't. It also makes most crewmembers happy because they know they are getting to go home pretty close to schedule. Having it live to tape also helps to create a better energy and excitement all around because nobody wants to mess anything up. When shows are just taped, they can run late, and sometimes hours after they are supposed to end. This was the case at the *VH1 Divas: A Tribute to Diana Ross* show I write about later in the Divas chapter.

## 14) Stage Manager

This is one stressful and important job! The stage manager is typically stationed backstage and off to the side. There can be any number of them, but usually around five. They are responsible for the flow of the show and making sure celebrities are on stage at the exact times they need to be. They coordinate everything that is happening on the stage with what the control booth (the area all the cameras feed through) and director wants. It is their responsibility to make sure the show runs smoothly and on time. Stage managers usually wear two sets of headsets, one for the backstage crew and the other to the control booth (the control booth usually uses another audio device they call the PL (Private Line) rather than the walkies most of the crew use). Having both devices allows them to get in touch with anyone they want. Can you imagine hearing twenty different people talking to you in one ear and another fifteen in the other, all while talking to people face to face? Ugh! This is a very difficult job and one mistake can make a huge impact on the show.

## 15) Camera Seats

In addition to show rundowns, the talent team can use a seating chart. The seating chart shows where each celebrity is seated in the audience. Sort of like a seating chart for a wedding. The venues have their own seating numbering systems, but many times they are not used because production usually takes out seats or rearranges previous seating layouts. Production's new seating layout is drawn up and has what are called, Camera Seats, labeled on it. These are the seats that are filled with celebrities. Camera people know what seats they are and will shoot coverage of those seats during the show. It is up to the talent team to make sure the celebrities are in the correct seats. If the seat is empty, it is up to the audience team to make sure someone is sitting in all of the seats. That is why when you watch a show you will rarely, if ever, see an empty seat. People are constantly rearranged so that this is possible.

The way the numbering usually works is the following. The house right section is usually A, and then there is B, and so on. Then the row closest to the stage is 1, followed by 2, etc. Then seats are numbers from house right to house left. No matter what the seats actually say, you need to follow the seating charts provided by production because the camera seats are what production follows.

Celebrity Photos or Place Cards are arranged in the seats that they will have for the show. These are good visuals for the crew to have when rehearsing. This picture was taken at a *Golden Globes* rehearsal.

## 16-17) House Left and House Right vs. Stage Left and Stage Right

These terms are all referring to direction. They can get confusing, so pay attention! This is the one thing new celebrity escorts always mess up and get confused about

When you sit in the audience, you will be facing the stage. If you draw an invisible line down the middle of the audience, the right side would be house right and the left side would be house left. Sounds simple right? Well if you were standing on the middle of the stage looking out to all the people sitting, to your right would be stage right and to your left is stage left. This is very simple; except people tend to get confused because stage left is house right and house left is stage right. Make sense? For instance, when a stage manager asks an escort to bring a celebrity, such as Angelina Jolie, from stage left to house right, the escort should bring her to the same side just to the audience area. Many new escorts would bring her to the wrong part of the audience or stage. All you need to do is to visualize them in either the house or on stage and then you can figure it out.

More mistakes are made because people lack knowledge of these terms, do not truly understanding them, or are in a hurry. If an escort is with their favorite star and they only have thirty-five seconds to get them to their seats, with people running all around and in their way, it can be difficult. Add fans vying for two seconds to talk to the celebrity and the noise of people talking on the walkie in your ear, it can be a challenge. But an escort CAN'T afford to make a mistake. If your job is to bring people to specific locations and you mess up, you probably won't have that job for very long. Like in most things in life, you can do ninety-nine percent of your job well and no one will notice, but you do one little thing wrong, it sticks out like a neon sign, especially when the results are broadcast on national television.

## 18-20) Green Room vs. Holding Room vs. Quick Change Room

Most shows have all three of these rooms, but there are a few shows that only have one or two of them. The Green Room is probably the most commonly referred to room and is used at every event. This is where celebrities and VIP guests can relax. It is usually filled with drinks, food, and a television monitor where they can watch what is happening live on stage. Green rooms are the most plush and luxurious rooms at the entire venue and are always guarded by security. On some shows, even the escorts are not allowed in, but this is mostly due to space limitations. Sometimes, the green room is used to hold the celebrity talent about fifteen minutes before they are supposed to appear on stage. However, many shows have a holding room for this very task.

A holding room is not as big or glamorous as a green room and is usually used to hold the talent for about ten to fifteen minutes before they are supposed to go on stage. This is the last chance to do touch ups on make-up, rehearse lines, or to just clear their head and work on their nerves. Many times this is not even a room, per say, but a tented area on the side of the stage that has a few chairs, some lights, and maybe a mirror. When the stage manager is ready for the talent to go on stage, he or she knows exactly where to find them because the escort has already pulled them into the holding room. It is seconds from where they need to be to enter the stage.

Every wonder how a host of a live show is able to change her dresses so quickly and look fantastic? That is because of the Quick Change Room! It is used mostly for hosts or singers who are performing multiple songs in a row. The room is a small-tented area backstage where the talent literally runs in, changes their clothing (with a lot of help from a small team of people) and runs out. Most times they don't have enough time to run back to their dressing room as it is further from the stage, which is why a quick change room is set up. Usually they have less than two to three minutes to run back, change their dress, touch-up their make-up and hair and get back into place on the stage. This is very stressful, but with a team full of talented people, it is easily done. When you watch shows now and notice the host is in a different outfit then before the commercial break, you will know what happens behind-the-scenes. Obviously, if it is not a live show they can take their time, but often the room is used to save production time and avoid any distractions.

## 21) Seat Fillers

A seat filler position is usually a volunteer opportunity that can be an exciting and fun experience for many people. It is a chance to see an award show for free and possibly sit next to or near your favorite celebrities. To me, I find it boring and literally feel unfulfilled after, but I have been very spoiled and lucky to do what I do. I tried it once after escorting for three years and I never wanted to do it again. Everyone else I speak to loves it because it is such a unique experience to get up close and personal with celebrities. Plus, you get to see a great show for free often times with the best seats!

This is how it works. At every televised award show, a group of people are brought in to sit in any empty seats that may appear on camera, because it would look strange, or at least less glamorous, to have them shown. They include celebrity seats. Throughout the show celebrities have to leave to go backstage, the bathroom, the green room etc. Once the celebrity gets up during a commercial break, a seat filler take sits. This is an exciting opportunity for many people because, although you usually don't meet the person you are seat filling for, you get to meet celebrities sitting in area and you also MAY have the opportunity to be seen on television.

The downside is when the celebrity returns, the filler must vacate and find another seat. This game of musical chairs many times leads you to no chair for a while and you have to stand in the back. But in most cases you still get to watch the show. Sometimes however, the celebrity doesn't come back because they want to stay backstage and the filler gets to stay for the evening. A seat filler never knows when and if they may need to get up. All changes only occur during commercial breaks except in the rare case of an emergency.

Production doesn't want to have to worry about seat fillers being late or not showing up and because of the high demand, often they have to arrive many hours before the show begins, which leads to a lot of standing around all dressed up. This especially sucks if you have to wait outside when it's hot and you are trying to stay looking sexy.

One quick fact: Eva Longoria was a seat filler before she became famous! I am not sure if she enjoyed it, but I am pretty sure she enjoys acting far better. Maybe fame does rub off!

**Relaxing after Rehearsals**

## 22) Pull

The term pull or pulling is used when someone, usually a stage manager or celebrity escort needs to get the talent from one location to another. For example, "Please pull Megan Fox in three minutes to the green room" means please go get Megan Fox in three minutes and bring her to the green room. Sometimes, especially on shows that are not live, a ten minute warning happens and the celebrity will still have to wait up to thirty or forty minutes because of unexpected delays. Many times the celebrity escort or stage manager will say they have a REAL ten minutes before being pulled. This means they are very confident the talent will be pulled in ten minutes with no delays. Sometimes there are still delays, but when the word REAL is added, the time frame is taken more seriously.

These are just a few of the basic terms used during every award show. There are so many others, but I wanted to introduce a few of them before you started to get too far into the book. I hope you found them interesting and useful.

# MY FIRST TIME

Most people remember their first thrilling experiences. You may recall your first kiss, your first roller coaster ride, or your first day of college as a bouquet of emotions. My first time working as celebrity escort has been etched into my mind. As it seems like it happened just yesterday. Escorting was like a cold breeze slapping against my face waking me up from the mundane life I was living. Don't get me wrong, I loved being twenty-four years old and working for MTV in New York City! I also had an incredible, loving family in Pennsylvania who thought I was crazy for living there. Even though I was only a few states away, I could feel their teeth grind because I had not pursued the legal career we all thought I would. The truth is, it would have been easier for me to go to law school and follow a nicely carved path. My parents even stated they would do whatever they could to help me achieve the goal of becoming a lawyer. I didn't follow that path because at the time, I was itching to explore the world before being engrossed with three more years of schooling. Besides, I could always go to law school, right?

Always having a love for movies, celebrities, and everything "Hollywood," I made the difficult decision to pursue entertainment. The closest and most obvious choice for me was to head to New York City. Though, I had only visited the city once when I was a child, I knew there was some television and film shooting there. Also, it was a short train ride home so frequent trips to see the family would be easy.

Besides, moving to Los Angeles seemed like an impossible dream because the distance from everything I loved was far too great. I recruited my best friend James to pack up his truck with my bare necessities. And so my adventure began.

**My First Visit to New York City
Please Note my Fashion Sense!**

Shortly after the big move, I was hardly paying the bills, very alone, confused about my life plans, and shocked how insignificant I felt in a city of movers and shakers. New York City has an enormous amount of great energy, but I just didn't have the road map to find my own way. Since ninth grade I was ready to take on the world, but I didn't realize so were hundreds of thousands of others. The elements I thought made me special and talented blended in with everyone else. Job opportunities were more like an emotional and intellectual gladiator competition. Finding a job was a task in itself. Without connections, even landing a temp job was a huge victory. After a few weeks, I scored that victory, though it paid me barely enough to cover my bills.

On the bright spring morning of Tuesday, April 13, 1999, I headed back to my tiny cubicle at MTV's Manhattan offices, that didn't feel like my own since I was only "temp" and there for such a short time. It wasn't the greatest of jobs for a twenty-four year old with a college degree and huge dreams, but still, at least I could say I was sort of working at MTV! As I sat down in front of the computer to do a mindless, very non-rock-n-roll task, a mid-level employee looking panicked caught my eye. Looking for anything to distract me from my duties, I watched as he frantically searched around the cubicles tossing papers and looking under a desk when he caught my stare. *Crap.* I was probably going to be thrown into some room to do some menial task this guy didn't want to do. I immediately put my head down and pretended to be busy at work, but he still approached me. *Great, here we go.* Doing my best to smile, I looked up at him with my optimal, "whatever you need" look. I was looking for full time work so I needed to come across as helpful. With a desperate look in his eyes, he leaned down to me and whispered,

"I need an escort for tonight, would you be interested?" Of course this caught me off guard, it's not every day you get asked to be an escort. Well, at least for me it wasn't. I couldn't believe he was asking me to sleep with someone for money! Was it to sleep with him? I may have been fresh off the proverbial turnip truck, the small-town Pennsylvania kid in the big city, but I wasn't about to become a midnight cowboy for anyone! *Why would he ask me?* I thought. My first reaction was to say, "I'm sorry, but I'm really not comfortable selling myself like that," but before I could answer, the man continued on--he must have noticed my deer in headlights look.

"It's for an award show, you would escort a celebrity." Then there was another awkward pause. He quickly realized what I was assuming and with a sly grin, he explained he needed an additional Celebrity Escort for the *VH1 Divas Live* music concert at New York's Beacon Theatre. I would greet celebrities, hang out on the red carpet, and have many other responsibilities he would explain later. Red carpets, Celebrities!!? I wanted to scream "Hell! Yes!" but instead I just nodded a quiet "yes". I'd never heard of such a job, but I would give it a shot.

The next thing I knew I was being given directions to the venue, told to find the "talent check in" (whatever the hell that was) and pick up an all-access credential. I was so new I didn't even know what a credential was. This was a lot to take in, but exciting at the same time. I reassured him I would be there. I knew I would at least go, but if anything became strange, I would immediately run screaming and probably laugh at myself later for being so naive. To this day, I don't know who that man was, or why he was walking around the floor or why he was searching through people's desks. But I have been eternally grateful that he did pop into my life for one brief moment. For the rest of that day at work I could not focus on anything as I wondered: *What celebrities I would meet? What it would be like to be on the red carpet? What exactly would happen?* And most of all, *what the hell would I wear?*

## *VH1 Divas Live* 1999, New York City

The evening had arrived and I had found something in my closet that looked cool enough to be worn at a VH1 event and it was black, the color of New York City nightlife's unofficial dress code. I was young and living in the city so club clothes were something I did have in abundance. If this had been a black tie event, I would have been completely screwed! Even though my cheap black club wear did match the style of what I was instructed to wear, I hoped they were good enough for this swanky event. My shirt was a simple black short sleeve with metallic silver snap buttons down the front, while my black pants had a glimmer of shine to them. All were form fitting and felt fun to wear. I spiked up my hair as I always had done, but I did spend an extra minute or two on it using hairspray to keep everything perfectly in place. Feeling I did all I could with what I had, I took a deep breath, popped in a piece of gum, and left.

As I got off at the nearest subway station, I kept reassuring myself this was probably all a big scam anyway, so I should stop wasting my time worrying about it. While I crossed seventy-second-street walking north on Broadway, I began to notice a crowd gathered ahead. *Maybe this is legit,* I thought. *This could actually be a real thing, but even if so, I still am not sleeping with anyone.*

When I reached the front entrance of the Beacon Theatre, I pulled out the crumbled piece of paper containing all the vital information and confirmed I was at the correct place. The huge sign made it obvious, but I needed to double check for some nervous reason. Little did I know at the time, but the Beacon Theatre has existed since the 1920's and was built for silent films. It has decades of rich art and history and I was about to experience a glimpse of it. On a normal day, I would have walked past it thinking it's some old building on the Upper West Side.

I slithered my way through the crowd of eager fans searching for someone that could help direct me when I noticed an overweight female security guard standing by the front door entrance as if she was guarding Buckingham Palace. She had the "I am official, but this is freaking cool" look on her face. I nervously mumbled the question "Where is Talent Check-In?" She, of course, had no idea what I was talking about and quickly dismissed me as if I was making something up to try to get past her. Instantly, I felt deflated. My jaw dropped and my heart sunk. *If she had no idea, it must be a big joke.* Just as I was about to walk away, another security guard who had overheard my question pointed and gruffly said it was just around the corner. The blood rushed back into my face and I quickly said thank you as I rushed off.

I turned the corner and I noticed across fans were gathered and looked as if they had been there for hours. There stood hundreds of people, very tired, but very eager, and committed to seeing someone famous before they would go on their way. Ropes held them back on that side of the street because this was the prime location--it was where the red carpet lay. My stomach dropped as I was overwhelmed by the amount of people and the tight security examining anyone who tried to enter.

A few feet away hung a sign that clearly read "Talent Check-In". Several people were standing in line when I joined in. It seemed as if it only took a second before it was my turn. Caught off guard, the woman sitting behind the table asked for my name and driver's license. I instantly froze. In shock and overwhelmed, I actually forgot my name and why I was there! Luckily, I quickly snapped out of it and said "Christopher Gaida. I am not a celebrity but here to escort them." She gave me the 'that's obvious stare,' took my license, and began to search for my name on a small list that already had most of them highlighted. Behind where the woman sat, crew people were running back and forth all looking busy. There was a buzz of energy and air of importance that rushed past me. Thankfully my name was on the list and after highlighting it, she gave me a plastic laminated card that had *VH1 Divas Live/99* printed on it, some tracking four digit number and a long rectangular like hole at the top with a thin metal beaded cord running through it. She called it a "credential" and said I had to wear it at all times. After struggling with the tiny metal clasp I was able to put it around my neck securely. I felt as if I had won an Olympic Medal. Somehow I felt validation by just wearing it, even though I didn't know what it was really for, or what I was supposed to do as an escort. I did feel a part of something big, I just didn't know how big.

I was told to head inside and the meeting probably had already begun. I knew by all the highlighted names I was one of the last to arrive, but I also knew I was not late. Regardless, my nerves tightened up at the thought of being the last to enter. After searching for about a minute, I found the group of escorts (maybe twenty-five people) gathered around one man, Jeff. He was clearly in charge, passing out maps and information about which celebrities would be attending and the layout for the evening. Still nervous and in shock, I approached the group like a middle school kid heading into the showers after gym class.

Jeff quickly welcomed me as he launched into a meeting that lasted a little over an hour. There was so much information told, I wished I had a note pad and pen to write it all down. I wasn't sure if I would remember it all, but no one else was taking notes so I hoped at least the important stuff would rub off. He used many foreign terms and explained we should not ask for autographs, pictures or phone numbers.

"This is a professional job and we need to act professional. There are lots of people watching us," he stated. Jeff was a middle-aged, balding man that clearly had done this before and I could tell he *lived* to be at these events. He was calm, kind and professional. I got the impression he may have been a nerd in high school, but now, as in many cases in life, he was the guy with the power many people wanted to know.

During the meeting everyone was assigned a celebrity. Jeff would call out an escort's name and then state which celebrity they were paired up with. When someone got a really popular celebrity, the other escorts would mumble and applaud. It was a happy, good for you, noise which I thought was interesting. There seemed to be no anger or resentment between the escorts, which is contrary to what you typically hear about the entertainment industry. I could tell already these people were very supportive of each other like a close loving family. After my name was called, I was shocked. Not because Jeff, like so many others, pronounced my last name incorrectly, but because I thought it being my first time, I was only going to just observe or escort an unknown. Instead, I was given three ladies from *Saturday Night Live* (*SNL*) who, at the time, were the exciting new flavor of the month: Cheri Oteri, Ana Gasteyer, and Molly Shannon. Although I had given up watching *SNL* years before, I was thrilled, but a bit overwhelmed knowing I had to escort all three! Escorting one person seemed difficult after hearing all the things we had to remember, but now I had three people to worry about. They were presenting and doing press together so I needed to make sure they stayed together.

Immediately after the meeting, we went on what is called a "walk through". We tour the entire place so we know where everything is and how to get to key places in a hurry. This can be the most confusing part of the job because different areas are not clearly marked or distinguished. Many times they start to look the same and you need to keep this huge blue print in your head. There was a paper map of the venue given to each of us, however, in a hurry they are very difficult to read and sometimes more confusing than just knowing the place well. Also, once a show starts, it is very easy to get rattled when there are fans around and other crew, moving equipment. Plus nerves can cloud and overwhelm an escort.

After completing our walk through, we had some free time before the red carpet opened. I was determined to do a great job because I realized what a privilege this experience was so I re-walked the entire route four or five times. I wanted to know every detail, where every door led, where every bathroom hid. I memorized the schedule down to the very second so my talent would have the best possible experience. One would think this might be an easy task, but I did not want to leave anything to chance. I also remembered the movie *The Bodyguard,* of which I am a big fan. If something bad would happen when a celebrity was on 'my watch', I wanted to be fully prepared to get us both to safety, immediately. I knew all of Kevin Costner's moves, so not only would I know how to save someone, I'd look cool doing it as well.

In addition to exploring the venue, I bombarded Jeff with specific questions he handled with great patience. I wanted to see if there had been any last minute changes or updates to the schedule. It may have annoyed him, but I'd rather ask early on then to get struck in a situation I could not handle or be confused. Finally, a bit before the event was to begin, I felt confident enough and was ready for the celebrities to arrive.

The evening was beyond anything I could ever express, except to say was fantastically magical. Celebrities kept arriving one after another looking as glamorous as when I watched these shows on television. This time though, I was a part of it! At one point, I turned around and stood within a few feet of Elton John, Cher, Mary J Blige, Tina Turner, Sarah Michelle Gellar and Ashley Judd. They were all there hanging like a group of college friends at a mixer. Everyone was not only accessible, but I could talk to anyone at any point about anything. Of course I said nothing, because I was extremely overwhelmed. I stood there soaking everything in and watching every move.

The line of reporters weaved for an amazingly long distance. The noise from people talking and taking pictures was almost deafening with the over powering level of energy and excitement. Everyone seemed enthralled to be at the event including the celebrities. Watching shows on television all these years I never wondered what the celebrities were actually thinking about. I did not question whether they were truly enjoying the events or just faking it for the camera. I stood in the midst waiting for my three ladies to arrive. I didn't know if they were coming together or separate and at what time they were to arrive. I was just told to wait at the top of the red carpet during this two-hour window and introduce myself when they got out of the limo.

As I stood nervously waiting, I hoped I would recognize them. It would be embarrassing if they walked past me and I continued to stand there like an idiot. I knew what they looked like, but *what if they dyed their hair, or wore a hat, or just looked different in person?* I also worried about what I would say and how I would introduce myself. My mind instantly flashed back to the scene we often see in television shows and films where a guy is about to go on a date and he rehearses what he is going to say in the mirror. I was replaying that scenario in my head, only I didn't have a mirror. Sadly, every line I came up with sounded lame.

Doubt quickly overtook my body like a spiritual possession. *Why would they want to hang out with someone like me? What if I get them lost? What if they don't like me? What if...? What if...? What if...?* rattled around in my head like a ghost in an attic. I took some deep breaths and reminded myself to remain calm. I needed to be in control and they were going to look for me to lead them. Time was flying by and the carpet became more and more crowded with celebrities and famous people of all levels. *I was a smart, nice guy and I could make this work.* I told myself.

While I eagerly waited, I noticed a bubbly blonde, LeAnn Rimes strutting down the red carpet in a sexy brown and white striped blouse. Closely by her side was her then boyfriend. I was amazed with how pretty she looked and remembered watching her on *Oprah* when she first started out her enormous singing career. She seemed so sweet and full of goodness, like a kindergarten teacher. As I watched her being interviewed by various reporters, I noticed her boyfriend was not really paying attention to her. As I watched closer, he checked other girls out. It wasn't that he just noticed the other women, but practically drooled over them. It annoyed me. I never met LeAnn or even saw her prior to this, but for some reason I felt very protective of her. It was an odd sense of loyalty. As they continued to go down the carpet, he continued to smile flirtatiously and stare at other women. I watched him like a hawk and it took every fiber of my being not to go to LeAnn and tell her what was happening behind her back. He was just looking and nothing more, but I was angry with him. Maybe he felt nervous being there or maybe he liked to people watch like I do? Maybe he wasn't flirting at all, but it just seemed wrong and I was upset.

*Who am I to say something? Why do I even care? Why am I all of a sudden the moral police and why does this bother me so much?* Maybe it was because she had no clue or maybe it was because I thought he should feel grateful to be there with her. This kind of stuff usually just rolls off my back, but at this moment I realized something very important: I was meant to do this job! I knew going forward I would make a great Celebrity Escort because I really cared about what was in the best interest of the celebrity. Not because I had judgmental thoughts or because it was something I had to do, but because I really wanted a person I never even met to be happy and to be treated with love, respect and honor. I was looking out for the talent it was instinctively part of me.

The time finally arrived. The *SNL* ladies climbed out of their limo. I walked over to them. I kept my introduction very short and shook their hands. It is hard for me to remember the exact words I did use to introduce myself because my brain was on another plane of existence. I felt as if I was having an out of body experience. I could hear everything is going on, but my brain felt so overwhelmed trying to process it all. It later became a big blur of what was said to whom. However, I do remember they were very charming and playful with their humor as they teased me for being nervous. I am sure I was a visibly shaking fool.

This was the first time for me to really meet a celebrity. I briefly met Susan Lucci in high school. I went with my mother to a QVC taping where she was selling her hair products. My mother had been a huge fan of the daytime drama *All My Children*. I also developed an addiction to it while watching it with her as she recovered from cancer. Meeting Susan was thrilling, but it was more of a brief hello and a quick picture rather than actually speaking with her. I was more than happy because I was tongue-tied. She had this glow of enormous beauty in person and it felt strange seeing someone on television at arm's length. I believe it did however make me truly realize these people are real and give me an adrenalin rush I hoped I could someday feel again. I had met the local weather caster when I was a child. I was so young that I barely remember it, besides, he wasn't really famous, to a child it seemed that way, but not to the rest of the world. Never had I had an opportunity to actually speak with a celebrity for more than one sentence, let alone spend hours with three of them, and now I was doing just that.

As we walked down the carpet, flashbulbs illuminated my face. I knew where to bring the ladies and what time to get them there. However, I was unsure of the little things, such as where to stand while with them on the carpet, how close I should be to them, do I talk to them, or not at all? All of a sudden, every little detail came up for question. So, I kept what I thought was a professional distance and tried to remain very proper. In other words, I was boring, stiff and quiet.

I continued my duties and handled everything backstage (more about details backstage in future chapters). At one point during the show, we went outside so one of them could smoke. They had a great rapport between them and they enjoyed spending time with each other. I stood there observing, trying to seem "professional," when Molly started to ask me a bunch of questions about myself. I slowly opened up to them and answered in brief responses, not really knowing how much to say. There were some quiet moments as cigarette smoke circled around me. Getting some courage, I finally asked, "How did you guys get started?" The dreaded question they had gotten numerous times, a question most celebrities rather not have to answer anymore. They politely explained the early days in their careers and then there was the dull silence again. I had nothing else to say or comment on. I was being a terrible conversationalist. The silence was quite apparent, so they started to talk again amongst each other. That was my moment to wow them, yet, I couldn't find anything to say.

In my mind, it was good enough to have met them and the fact I actually spoke with them, was amazing. All this on top of seeing everyone on the red carpet and being backstage was enough to talk about with my family and friends for weeks! If I were going to continue working as an escort, I couldn't let anyone know I was so easily star struck. I would need to treat celebrities as people first. I only hoped I would be given another opportunity to escort.

Little did I know at the time this one experience was going to open the door for me to work on over one-hundred and fifty award shows and benefits for well over a decade--making me one of the top celebrity escorts in the world.

# RED CARPET SECRETS

The word "Hollywood" means many different things to people. It's the Hollywood sign, the Walk of Fame, Beverly Hills, swimming pools, and palm trees. However most people instantly think of fortune, celebrities and the exclusive Red Carpets. For decades people from all walks of life have gathered in front of their televisions, tuned in to watch celebrities arrive at the most glamorous of events. Magazines cover everything from fashion, to who is dating whom. It seems all is on display and secrets are revealed during this short walk. Break ups are apparent, pregnancies are unveiled, and even the few extra pounds, gained or lost, are on display and criticized for days after the event. You would think everything has been discussed, however, there are a few secrets and interesting things the media has not covered. These alluring facts will hopefully paint a more accurate picture of this world and the amount of work needed to create the magical moments you see on television.

Each year it seems that red carpets have become a show unto itself. In many cases, a show has its own prime-time spots before the actual event. Much of the time spent is focused on superficial desires such as "who" is wearing what and "who" looks better then who. Prior to the 1980's, celebrities just went to the store to buy a new dress or sometimes wore what they already had in their closets (the horror!). Now, there are dozens of media outlets throughout the world recording

**The View of a Red Carpet from Behind the Reporters and Cameras**

their arrivals and getting interviews on their latest projects making this a fashion driven circus sometimes lasting over two hours! For me, it's one of the best parts of the evening however, what's happening behind-the-scenes while this is going on is a world of itself.

With that being said, let me now take you behind the velvet rope and onto the red carpet for a behind-the-scenes look very few people ever get to see. Here are several secrets of the red carpet....

**Secret Number 1:**

First off, in order to even become close to sticking a foot on this highly publicized rug, you need something simple, a credential. Obtaining a credential is the hard part because you have to be working on the show and they are kept under close supervision. In most cases, if you lose your credential, you will not be given a new one and will not be able to work. Security cannot afford to have extra credentials floating around. There are many people with these plastic passes dangling from their necks as they run in different directions and usually, each one of them has a job. Many times these credentials will include a small photo of the person's face to whom it belongs. Otherwise, sneaky people will give their pass to a friend so they can get a glimpse of the excitement. My picture always seems to look like a bad Department of Motor Vehicles photo. Why I never get a good picture on these things is beyond me!

All of these people with credentials DO NOT have access to the carpet. Everyone needs one in order to even come close to the venue. The red carpet is even stricter. Unless your job function requires your skills on the carpet, you are not allowed on it. Every person's credential is coded differently depending on his or her job responsibilities, and it is clearly stated on them where you are allowed to go. Most times there are certain code letters such as the HPOEDAR listed above. I usually have no idea what the letters mean, but I know if someone is missing a certain letter, then security will not allow them in certain areas. Sometimes the credential is just coded by having a general category such as "Crew", "Celebrity Escort" or "Red Carpet Pre-Show" printed on it. Other shows have the actual credentials as different colors. It is up to the security to know which categories/credentials have access and which do not. They are all given credential sheets with this coding that helps remind them of the restrictions. Often these sheets are posted by the security stations.

As far as escorts, we don't need to worry about all of the details because we usually get a credential allowing *All Access* at each show. This is a rare and special privilege! The majority of people are not that lucky. For example, most reporters have a code for just the red carpet and do not have access backstage or any other exclusive areas such as the green room. And even on the carpet they are typically corralled to a small area they can't leave. Some reporters are not even able to go in to see the show. Other people such as production assistants or the lighting crew may be restricted from the red carpet and only have backstage access.

Celebrities are rarely given credentials, but when they are, the escorts hold those them for the entire evening. In essence, the escort becomes their credential if they are not recognized for who they are. Who wants to see a star sporting the latest fashion with a big plastic badge around their necks? If a celebrity is not recognized by security, the escort is there to make sure they are given access. In addition, even if a recognized celebrity is trying to get into a restricted area, such as backstage, and doesn't have an escort, they are not able to. Security knows without a credential or an escort, NO ONE is allowed in these areas. This is a common rule and sometimes is a bitter pill to swallow for some.

**Secret Number 2:**

High profile shows such as the *Academy Awards* have a microchip impeded into the credential, which makes security as tight as possible. When a person reaches certain checkpoints they have to have their credential scanned by security personnel. It will then register on a computer whether you are allowed access or not. Your entrance and exit times will also be recorded so producers and security know at what time you accessed what areas. All this for people who have a credential! Most shows are not this strict and have the security personal positioned at various points as well as roaming always checking for proper credential coding. This is usually sufficient enough for lower profile award shows.

**Secret Number 3:**

Just having a credential does not make the venue safe enough. Before you are to arrive for work, every crewmember is given a parking pass for the dashboard of their car. This is sometimes mailed or given out in meetings prior to the event; however, at some shows it has been e-mailed to me. When celebrities arrive in their limos each vehicle has a specific pass as well, even if they are just dropping someone off at the front door.

At the larger shows such as *The Grammy's*, every car is searched before allowing access to park. Barricades have been set up in an obstacle course way so no car can race through the checkpoint. Cars line up one by one while security checks credentials as well as searches the trunk of each vehicle. When all clear, they then have a long pole with a mirror on the end to stick underneath each car to help search for car bombs. Once cleared you continue to drive around these barricades until you reach the parking garage. After all this, finding parking is usually a breeze!

A large show such as the *Grammys* have streets blocked off and cement barricades set up. People attending or working the show have to drive around these after passing a security check point.

**Secret Number 4:**

The *Academy Awards* places snipers on rooftops of surrounding buildings, as well as heat seeking devices to look for weapons from a distance. With all of this security you would think I would feel safe, but personally it made me more paranoid. Especially because I start to wonder why they *need* all that security!

**Secret Number 5:**

Even before a red carpet starts, and before celebrity escorts arrive, there are required preparations. For some award shows, crews work months, even all year planning, preparing and building things…all for one night of glitz and glam.

These chandeliers lay on the sidewalk of the Beverly Hilton Hotel as well as other supplies. They are waiting to be hung inside for one of the many parties that evening. So much work to make the evening magical.

There is the obvious day before and the day of when everything needs set up. There is also the day or two before where they block traffic by shutting down a lane or two (in Los Angeles people LOVE that). If it is the *Academy Awards* it's the entire street because the red carpet is actually on Hollywood Boulevard.

There are measurements, plans, permits, lighting, arrangement of reporters, etc., but there are other small things I thought were interesting. For example, it amazed me the first time I saw someone vacuuming the red carpet. It's just something you never think of! It makes sense they need to make sure the carpet is perfect looking--it just never occurred to me they actually vacuumed it. All the preparation takes hours and sometimes days for a carpet to get set up with all it entails.

**I never ever thought the carpet got vacuumed. So funny to me!**

Another interesting thing to see is a perfect official NBC sign up close or a giant statue of an Oscar getting its butt painted or touched-up. It is actually someone's job to touch-up the giant gold statues and channel logos. On TV it's just something you see in the background and don't think much of it, but in reality, that one object took months of planning, building, painting, and installing.

**Secret Number 6:**

About two hours before an award show begins, the red carpet is officially "open" and arrivals start. Usually it is very slow for the first hour and then towards the end of the second hour, everyone arrives at the same time causing the typical mash-up. Reporters are in place and many tape quick clips for their pre-shows. Escorts are lined up in a certain area around the area, usually at the top (beginning) eagerly waiting for their talent to arrive. In another area, close-by, (sometimes referred to as the publicists holding pin), publicists impatiently wait as they constantly call their talent to make sure he/she is getting in the car on time. Sometimes we wait around for almost the entire two hours as many celebrities are fighting traffic or waiting to make a grand entrance. Some interviews taped early on the carpet are played LIVE later to fill in dead air space.

Celebrities that do not want to do the red carpet will arrive in a back entrance where an escort will wait. We are usually told this in advance so we can be prepared logistically.

**Secret Number 7:**

Once the celebrity does arrive, the escort introduces or greets them and their guest(s) and together they begin to walk the carpet. On most shows, the limo arrival area is where this introduction occurs. The network airing the main pre-show usually has one camera that catches these moments. Then they are funneled into a tented area where everyone, that's right, EVERYONE needs to go through security mags. Mags, is short for Magnetometer. They are electronic walk through metal detectors similar to the type you go through in airports. Obviously, you don't see this on TV! Even celebrities are required to go through the metal detectors. Yes, that includes Justin Bieber who tried to avoid them at an *MTV Video Music Awards* show. His security and the security at the venue got into a little scuffle because Justin did go through but continued walking after the mags went off. His security was rushing him in and tried to get past venue security. Venue security won and the only outcome from this was him emptying his pockets, getting wand and people having to wait longer to go through.

Under the tents are the Mags for the *Primetime Emmys* for both guests and celebrities. Cameras are usually not pointed in this direction so you would never know.

Michael Douglas and Catherine Zeta-Jones going through the Mags

The mags are only placed at the entrances so once you go through you don't have to do it again for the rest of the show. The only exception would be if you exit and enter the unsecured area again. Even if you leave the secured area to say hello to someone for five seconds and security can see you only a few feet away, you are still required to go through them again. This is sometimes difficult when you need to greet the celebrity outside of the mags area and walk them in. Celebrity escorts usually have their mics and radios on and under their clothing so these need to be disconnected and taken off and put in a bucket so you can walk through. Many times you will get a nice security person who will use their wand to scan you and double check it is the radio setting off the detector.

**Secret Number 8:**

After clearing security, the Stars have one last chance to adjust everything before going out in public and being photographed. Typically there is a mirror in the security tent for this reason. Once they leave that tent, they are greeted by dozens of photographers lined up in a row. This is the still photo section of the carpet where celebrities walk a few steps and pose and continue doing this down the line until they reach the end. It is also referred to as the step and repeat, for obvious reasons. As they do this, the photographers go crazy yelling at the celebrities to look their way so they can be the person with the most perfect shot. I usually follow a few steps behind giving them subtle clues to keep moving down so things keep flowing smoothly. If I become even a little too close to the celebrity on this part of the carpet, photographers shout for me to get out of their shot. They can be vicious! They are like angry lions wanting their dinner and I'm the pesky branch in the way of their meal. The publicists typically stand next to me or in some occasions take the lead and slowly pull their talent along the line. It always amazes me that the same groups of photographers are at show after show, and yet they often yell and scream at each other while to get the best shot. It's a tough, competitive business and the best picture gets the most money, so they will do what they have to get it. I have even seen many elbows thrown in anger, I'm always waiting for a full fledge fistfight to break out between the paparazzi.

A view from the *Emmys* carpet before everyone arrives.
How awesome it is to be standing there!

It takes a good deal of energy for these celebrities to pose and smile while making sure they look their best. Especially when they know one sneeze, sniff or frown is the picture the paparazzi may put in a tabloid saying how miserable they looked. That's a lot of stress. I even feel like I am under a microscope during this, even though no one cares who I am. The step and repeat area of the carpet can take a celebrity up to ten minutes to walk through depending on how long the celebrity wants to stay and pose. It's a very short distance, just lots of photographers. When I was with Megan Fox at an event, her publicist brought her through it in less than ten seconds! I was shocked and a bit disappointed because I wanted to "accidentally" be photographed with her.

Immediately after the still photographer/step and repeat section comes the longest section of the carpet, what the viewer's mostly see on television. Lined on one side of the carpet are reporters and camera people hoping to speak with specific celebrities. They don't want just anyone or all of the celebs, they each have lists of who they would like to speak to, what questions to ask, and some research on them. Many have a backup list, in case they are not able to catch the attention of the celebrity they are after. If I were a reporter, I would become friendly with the escorts so they could help strategically navigate a celebrity towards me. Celebrities have so many reporters to choose from and can't do them all. Having someone on the "inside" would make things much easier.

**Secret Number 9:**

Cheat sheets. At the feet of each of the camera people are white pieces of paper that are taped to the carpet with the name of the show they are from printed on them. I like to call them cheat sheets. These pieces of paper make it much easier for everyone to determine whom they are and whether that particular celebrity would like to do an interview with them. These interviews are exhausting and most celebrities can only do a handful because of the limited time, cramped space, and many times hot weather. You might not think talking about yourself to someone is hard, but try it in five-inch heels, or a skintight suit in one hundred-degree temperatures. Then on top of that, add people yelling at you from every direction, including fans from the bleachers lined up behind you. The celebrity also knows they need to be inside in time to prepare. They also have a long evening still ahead of them. And all this is after hours of getting ready--trust me, it's exhausting. Sure it's not as serious as feeding your starving children, but one bad pose can lead to a month worth of bad press and lack of employment.

**Secret Number 10:**

One secret award shows and celebrities tend to keep hidden from the public is how the stars actual arrive for an evening of glitz and glamour. Many times the celebrities are *already* at the show and have been for hours before you see their "arrival" on camera. Some celebrities have rehearsal times the day of the show and things usually run late so they actually stay at the show's venue instead of running home. Celebrities still want to make their grand entrance so their arrivals are sometimes manufactured a bit by sneaking out the back door, driving around to the red carpet area, and then acting as if they had just arrived. This is obviously not preferred by the celebrity however sometimes it is just a necessity. Here is one of those instances…

## *Extreme Sports Awards* 2007 - Burbank, CA

When I visited France a few years back, I stayed at the Paris Hilton. But despite my numerous celebrity handlings never had I expected to meet and escort THE Paris Hilton. Who hasn't heard of this hotel heiress? She's sexy, popular, scandalous, and not someone I would want on my team when playing Trivia Pursuit, but very sweet. Paris and I were at the venue for her rehearsal the afternoon of the event. It became late in the day, making it very close to the red carpet start time. Instead of running all the way home to change, she decided to have her wardrobe and make-up person come to her dressing room to glam her up at the venue.

However, Paris still wanted to walk the red carpet and make her presence known. After about an hour of finishing touches, we sat in her dressing room and purposely waited until the final fifteen minutes before the close of the red carpet. She did not want to be the first to arrive and I guess enjoys the drama of being one of the last to "arrive". I think most celebrities do because they feel it makes them appear busy and more important. When I am an escort waiting for talent to arrive, I just think it is annoying.

During this down time, I searched the building and located a back door where I asked the black SUV to be positioned waiting for us. This area was very safe and hidden from both the public and reporters so I knew Paris and her team would be happy. I quickly became very anxious because I knew only fifteen minutes remained. It would be difficult to pull this off and have her do all the interviews I thought she would want to do. I asked several times for us to leave and finally her manager said they were ready to go. I prayed the limo driver did as I asked and was ready for us since I was not able to double check in time. I quickly led her manager, security guard, and Paris down the halls to the back door where we snuck out, loaded into the car, and drove around the building.

**Paris Hilton and I Enjoying the After Party**

Forty-five seconds later we arrived just as if she came from home! No one was the wiser. I was sitting in the front seat and exited while someone from the transportation department opened her door for her. She stepped out in all of her glory and together we all headed down the carpet. Ready for an onslaught of interviews, Paris's manager told me they were going to quickly do the carpet. Unsure of what he meant, I took her lead and was surprised to find out we all just raced down the carpet not stopping to do any interviews at all. I was a little dumbfounded by having us wait all that time and then run through without doing any press. We may have stopped once, but it's hard to recall if it was to answer one quick question or we were held up for some reason. I guess this was a strategy of showing she was at the event without having to answer possibly difficult questions?

It's something you would never think of when watching stars get out a limo. People think these shows are so easy and celebrities come from home after relaxing all day and it's all a 'simple life.' They don't realize how busy things can be and how tight schedules many times are. If Paris had gone home first she would never have made it in time for any red carpet appearance and may have been late for the show as well. However, she did have time to talk to the press, but I am still not sure why they choose not to. Whatever their reasoning, they know what they are doing because practically everyone knows who Paris Hilton is.

As a side note, getting out of a limo with a celebrity never gets old for me--even if I was in the front seat and it was for work. I think it's a blast to be seen as one of their friends or peers and I love when pictures float around the Internet capturing these moments for me. As nerdy as it may sound, I guess it's a little feeling of justice from NOT being cool in high school. It really means nothing in life, but I guess for people watching I imagine they wish they could be in the front seat, and for one second I am cool.

The rest of the evening went very well. Spending the day with Paris was much different than I expected because we had very little to talk about. She had her one-liners (which I always think of as funny), but I was hoping to find this well-read woman who acted as if she was a dim socialite for the cameras (a little brighter, complex?). That did not happen. What I found was a rich, sweet and fun girl who really only wanted to have fun. She was not one of those 'mean girls', but just a pampered, kind person looking for the next party. One thing I did find interesting about Paris was that she smoked an incredible amount of cigarettes, but was so nervous of letting anyone see her do it. I am not sure why she didn't want people to know, but she did hide it well with the numerous amount of gum she consumed during the course of the evening, and the consistent spraying of perfume. In fact, when we were in the SUV heading towards the red carpet, we actually stopped before rounding the corner so that she could have a few puffs of a cigarette. It has been a few years so I hope she has stopped that bad habit since then.

Before she was about to leave, Paris did take the time to come over and thank me for my help. Many celebrities rush off and some even forget or don't bother saying good night. I know it gets busy at the end of an event, but if someone helps you for several hours, the least you could do is say goodbye. Paris not only went out of her way to come over to wish me goodnight, but she unexpectedly smooched me on my check. I quickly became embarrassed because there were lots of people around and I am sure several guys were jealous. It was extremely sweet of her. I felt like the Hotel Manager in the movie "Pretty Woman" when Vivian told him he was very cool. How many people can say they got kissed by Paris Hilton?!

**Secret Number 11:**

Typically the weather is warm and sunny in Southern California, where many award shows take place. However, some days are just hot while other days are blazing! Most people forget Los Angeles is a desert. Add formal wear, make-up, the sun beating down with camera lighting pointed at you, and it's amazing people don't melt on the spot. Yes, on television it may look fun and alluring. You see all of these stars looking perfect, sexy, and carefree as they give interviews along the carpet. So how do they do that if it truly can be hot?

I never knew myself until one day I noticed something very interesting. There I stood, sweating in my tuxedo, as my skin seemed to boil from this Los Angeles heat wave we were having. I wiped my brow with a wad of paper towels I took from the bathroom and thinking if I were a celebrity, I wouldn't want to do any interviews because I would not only feel terrible, but look like a drenched, smelly rat. Then the answer came to me as I carefully watched an interview several feet from where I was standing. While celebrities were being interviewed, several reporters had a portable air conditioners pointed on the talent to keep them cool! *Genius*, I thought as I saw the older gentlemen struggle to hold onto this huge tube of cold blowing air. It looked very refreshing and although the celebrities did not have it following them between interviews, it gave them some quick bursts of relief. This certainly isn't something reporters report about and it is not outright obvious by watching the red carpet on television. It is a little secret of Hollywood I found interesting. It is very smart for a reporter to have because if I was a celebrity, I would head to the reporters with AC blowing before anyone else. Some days, I wish I could have one of those machines follow me around all the time.

**Red Carpet Air-Conditioning**

I guess some celebrities are just naturally cool though, because Susan Lucci didn't seem to sweat a bit when strutting her stuff at the *Daytime Emmys* in 2008. I was escorting her in Hollywood when it was almost a hundred degrees and the sun was directly beating down on the red carpet. Her publicist held an umbrella up, trying to keep everyone cool, but I still was a sweaty mess! Susan said she was hot, but did her interviews and didn't look at all bothered by the terrible heat.

**Secret Number 12:**

While the term "red carpet" is synonymous with a long red carpet, it doesn't necessarily mean it has to be red. Some shows have different colors to signify different things. For example, the *Kids Choice Awards* has orange and shows like the *Independent Spirit Awards*, *Do Something! Awards*, and *CMT Music Awards* all have chosen blue. Even though they are a different color, people still call them "red carpets". The two words themselves have been turned into more of a term than a literally meaning. If you say red carpet to anyone, they immediately have a picture in their head of what you are talking about. I'm willing to bet no one would just picture a red living room carpet when you say that term to them! While some award shows try to have fun with their color and say, "the blue carpet", regardless, it's still the red carpet to everyone.

**Secret Number 13:**

It's New Year's Eve and you are curled up on the couch with a loved one about to toast in the New Year. You have *Dick Clark's New Year's Rockin' Eve with Ryan Seacrest* on and you watch all these people partying in Times Square. They then flash to people in Los Angeles living it up and someone's performing. They flashback to NYC again to the countdown. 3, 2, 1 Happy New Year. Everyone goes crazy in New York. They flash to LA and everyone goes crazy there as well celebrating the start of another year. What you may not know is the Los Angeles party happenings, actually happened a month ago! That's right, it was taped several weeks prior to New Years. The live portion of this program is the happenings in Times Square, the rest has been taped. Now this may not, and probably should not, matter to you since the show is a classic, but my point to this is that not all aspects of shows are LIVE. The show may say it is live, but some elements are taped well in advance. It would be very difficult to shoot everything at once, and more difficult to book all of these performers for a major day like New Year's Eve. If the words LIVE appear on the screen, then those segments are live, if they are not then assume they are taped. I thought it was funny when I had escorted Fergie at this show one year and we were screaming "Happy New Year" in early December. All of those people celebrating were probably sitting home on New Year's watching themselves.

I want to do a shout out to Fergie because she, Josh, and her family were so awesome to me while I escorted her at this New Year's Eve taping. I actually left before Fergie on the day of taping, and she was so sweet that she offered me a limo ride to my car parked a few blocks away.

# RED CARPET UNROLLED

Having escorted over a hundred red carpet events, I have countless stories to tell about the trials and tribulations of a celebrity escort. If I were to tell all the stories, this book would be thicker than a dictionary. Therefore, I have to be choosy and only tell the stories I find particularly interesting or have special meaning to me. Below are some of my proudest moments, funniest stories, and interesting tales from the red carpet.

## 78th Annual Academy Awards 2006 - Hollywood, CA
## 80th Annual Academy Awards 2008 - Hollywood, CA

Out of every award show, there is only one that sits on top as the undisputed biggest in the world, the *Academy Awards*. The most grand, most exciting, most watched event of the year, and I was asked to escort celebrities down its glorious red carpet. Standing on the red carpet of the *Academy Awards* in Hollywood has to be one of the proudest moments in my life. It was truly an amazing, surreal experience.

About two weeks before the *Oscars*, I received an e-mail asking if I would be interested in handling celebrity logistics for the red carpet. I would have to be there for a meeting a few days before the show, for rehearsals the day before and then of course the entire day of the show. I immediately responded yes. I was also asked not to tell other escorts about this opportunity because they were only able to invite a few of the best to work on it. I guess they didn't want to deal with other escorts feeling snubbed. I was, of course, thrilled to work the event and had to give my social security number as well as other personal information to pass a background check. Since murder and crime is not my thing, I knew all would turn out well so I instantly called my parents and best friend to tell them the good news.

Time flew by quickly. I attended the mandatory meeting, and the Saturday rehearsal one-day prior. I learned would not be doing the normal escorting job, but instead I would be responsible for keeping celebrities moving along the carpet. With so many people and a tight time frame, I would need to make sure there were no mistakes. Certain celebrities needed to be at previously agreed upon interviews. At the start of the show certain celebrities had to be in their seats--as the host would be mentioning their names. I also needed to make sure people were moving on the carpet to avoid a traffic jam of talent in one section. I was very confident about doing the job since it seemed easier than my normal tasks as a celebrity escort.

Show day arrived. I stood there in the midst of the *Academy Awards* red carpet! I had watched this show every year while growing up in Pennsylvania, but getting to actually be there...it was beyond words. Hell, who doesn't watch the *Oscars*? Besides the Super Bowl, it typically has one of the largest viewing audiences in the world, year after year.

The best of the best actors all gathered together to honor each other and the creative genre of storytelling. All of these thoughts ran through my head as I waited for the A-listers to arrive. I appreciated every second of it and thought about how far I had come. I absorbed every moment, making sure to lock these memories in my mind forever.

I was so proud to actually touch an Oscar! Of course this was the day of rehearsals so both Oscar and myself still needed to spruce up a little.

With my feet planted squarely on the red carpet, I looked up at the beautiful blue sky, closed my eyes and took a deep breath as I fought back tears. Trying to distract myself from being a blubbering mess, I looked at the teams of security on the roofs of surrounding buildings, and even saw helicopters patrolling above. I looked down the carpet seeing people arrive with big bright smiles on their faces. Whether it was a celebrity, guest or even an assistant, everyone glowed with excitement. With my back to the Kodak Theatre, I looked across Highland Avenue to the far side of the street and saw hundreds of people lined up in hopes of just getting a glimpse of a celebrity arriving. Everyone appeared to burst at the seams with anticipation.

As soon as ANY limo door opened, cameras went off. While standing there watching the countless number of people surrounding me, I realized millions of others watched us on this red carpet. Children were dreaming of one day walking it in hopes to receive an award, adult's critiqued dresses, fans ogled their favorite stars, people were sexually fantasying about their favorite actors while others dreamed of just getting a handshake from one; and I was right in the middle of it. All of the years of watching on television and I hoped to have an opportunity to be on a red carpet… and here I was, ready to guide some of the most famous and talented people in the world down the biggest and best red carpet. I could feel my perspective and goals in life shift. Just like for some celebrities, this red carpet was literally their path to an Oscar, something would be life changing for them as well. And so it was for me.

**My view of the *Academy Awards* Red Carpet.
I was dressed and ready for the stars to arrive.**

Getting celebrities down the red carpet swiftly and into the Kodak Theatre before the start of this live telecast quickly became a more challenging task than I had anticipated. This was their moment. I didn't want to rush them along as if they were voyeurs of a car accident. There were cameras pointing in every direction and the talent team was told to make sure we always looked busy because everyone (especially the producers) was watching. If we goofed off, someone would see it. I, of course, didn't need that lecture. I understood the gravity of this opportunity and had an array of experience, so I was used to the drill. It was a good reminder though, because I could see any one of us getting sucked into the excitement.

One of the duties I was assigned to was to direct specific celebrities to three different stages on the red carpet, at exact times for the pre-show and its producers. There was a list of celebrities who already agreed to be interviewed at those specific times. This added to the chaos because we never knew when someone would arrive. I scanned the list of celebrities and when I saw Cameron Diaz's name, I jumped at claiming her as one of my responsibilities. I had always wanted to meet her because she has this sexy sweet allure to her that makes me want to be her best friend. I was hoping that would be the case in person as well.

As the minutes passed, the carpet flooded with sea of the rich, beautiful, and botoxed. It could not get more exciting; everywhere I looked was a famous movie star, but from a distance they all started to blend together. As I carefully shuffled the stars down the carpet, the chatter on my walkie gave me a headache. Everyone needed something right away. The constant announcements of celebrity names roared constantly. I had to listen closely though, because if someone asked for me and I didn't respond, that would be the kiss of death for this job. Things were frantic when I heard through my earpiece Cameron had arrived. Without trying to look like I was in a hurry, I headed to greet her. People were so packed in, I had to zig and zag as if I was a running back going for a touchdown.

Finally there, I caught my breath and introduced myself to Cameron and her publicist Brad. They wanted to start doing interviews immediately because we all felt packed in like sardines. Just after about three interviews, it was announced on my walkie the schedule had changed. They needed Cameron Diaz at Stage Three in seven minutes. That of course was the exact opposite end of where we were standing and she was in the middle of an interview already. I told my supervisor she had just arrived and I didn't think we could make it in time. I was told that it was not an option. She *had* to be there.

Quickly explaining the situation to her and Brad, I rushed them down the carpet. Reporters shouted at us, thinking we were skipping them and the interview they wanted with her. I tried to explain we would come back, but everything was so loud I doubt they heard what I was saying--I certainly didn't have time to stop. Cameron told me she hoped they didn't think she was being rude, as she seemed pretty uneasy about skipping to the end of the carpet. Seeing her unrest, I reassured her they would understand. This interview was important and we would go back to where she had left off. I quickly started to part the sea of people on the far outside lane of the red carpet so the reporters and cameras were less likely to see her race by. This meant we were very close to the stand where hundreds of fans stood shouting to get her attention and a quick wave. My walkie repeatedly went off several times asking me for an update on the status about every 30 seconds or so, all the while Brad was asking me why this had to happen now. It was stressful to say the least.

I did my best to assure him we could return to the beginning of the carpet after this stage interview and he seemed content with that. With less than thirty seconds to spare, and me now in a deep sweat, I delivered Ms. Diaz to the manager of Stage Three for the interview. The pressure in these situations can get extremely intense. All of this is just part of my job and I am proud to say I have always delivered perfectly. After the interview, I walked Cameron and Brad back to the top of the red carpet. They both thanked me for my help. Cameron was very sweet and her giddy, fun personality that comes across in many of her movies is the real deal. I sadly had to leave them to escort a few other celebrities, but Cameron was definitely my personal highlight.

On a side note, there are only a handful of publicists I think are incredibly talented AND kind people. Brad is one of them. I don't know him personally, but every time I have worked with him he treated everyone with such great respect. He was always a positive, happy person. Thank you both for making my *Oscars* experience even better!

## VH1 Divas: An Honors Concert for the Save the Music Foundation 2002 - Las Vegas

Ever since the movie *Goonies* came out, I have loved Cyndi Lauper's music. It's fun, upbeat, and her strong voice is incredible! When I heard she was going to need an escort to the *VH1 Divas* show in Las Vegas, I decided to drive out there with my best friend/dog, Oliver. Oliver and I had moved to Los Angeles a month prior and everything was new and exciting, including a trip to Vegas. We had spent one brief night in Vegas while driving across country from New York City to Los Angeles, but, I really had no time to soak in the city.

73

This time, I decided to go a day earlier so I could embrace the city and test my chances at winning on the quarter slots.

As an added bonus, I knew Oliver would enjoy the many unique smells during his daily walks. The production company was not paying for a room so I found a cheap place that accepted dogs directly across the street from the venue. When I say cheap, I definitely got what I paid for. Ugh!

The show took place at the MGM Grand Casino located on the main Las Vegas strip. The place is massive, so I made sure to walk through all the areas we needed to know numerous times the day before, and morning of, the show. Because most of the celebrities were staying at the hotel, we were directed to meet them at a specific service elevator to sneak them outside where the limos would be waiting. It was a smart decision because we would encounter less of the general public this way. The limo would then drive us around the casino to where the red carpet was laid out and the celebrities could make their grand entrance for press and fans. Sounds silly since they're already in the building, but without having a grand entrance and a red carpet, what is an award show?

While waiting for Cyndi at the service elevator on the ground floor, I decided to double check for her limo and confirm the area was still secure. It's funny because we were only around the corner from the red carpet, but we couldn't have the celebrities walk over to it, they *had* to arrive by limo. They needed the red carpet arrival experience for the fans. It was also very hot outside (hello...Vegas) and a short walk could ruin a stars make-up job. Luckily this show had a less formal dress code so my tuxedo remained hanging in my closet in Los Angeles in exchange for a more breathable outfit. Instead, I wore a pair of shiny black club pants and a short sleeve hip black club shirt--something I had worn at two other shows now. I hoped because this show was in Vegas many of the people attending would be different, and those who were the same would not notice. I had spent too much on gas and a hotel room to afford another outfit. My days of buying and returning clothes were a thing of the past.

The red carpet had already begun when Cyndi and her longtime publicist came out of the elevator both looking gorgeous. I introduced myself and all three of us climbed into the back of the limo. Within seconds Cyndi had me cracking up with her wit and charm. I couldn't help but tell her she should star in a sit-com because she was so funny. She explained she tried in the 1980s, but unfortunately the show didn't catch on.

After a few minutes, the drive seemed to be lasting longer than it needed to, and there was no red carpet in sight. We had been so wrapped up in a conversation about her experience recording the classic 1985's charity single, "We Are the World", none of us had watched in what direction the limo drove. I questioned the driver and he said even though the carpet was close to where we were, he was directed to go around the casino in the opposite direction due to traffic patterns. Shrugging it off I used this opportunity to babble on about some other things with Cyndi, including how incredible it must have been to be a part of that historical moment.

Several more minutes passed and we still had not arrived at the carpet. I became really concerned. "We were probably only two-thousand feet from the red carpet and how could a drive take almost ten minutes?" I asked. The driver said he thought it was right around the next corner. I was new to Vegas, but looked out the window to try and see where we were at this point, sadly it all looked the same to me. The good thing is we were still on the MGM Grand property, just lost along the hotels many sides. Then I noticed Cyndi and her publicist starting to become impatient. I commented, "At least we are in air conditioning," but that did little to ease the tension.

I firmly asked the driver once again where we were and when were we going to get there. He said the most dreaded words I could imagine, "I'm not quite sure where it is. I'm lost." My heart dropped. "Lost?" I responded. "All you had to do was drive to the side of the building. How on earth could you get lost?" I said calmly as I manage. It was my job to get Cyndi to the red carpet and this guy was going to make me look bad. The driver started to radio in that he not sure where to go. I looked out the window, once again, and the hotel was still on our left, so how lost could we be?

I was about to go on a rant about, "how could someone whose job it was to drive in this city for living not know how to make it a few hundred yards?" when Cyndi said the most unexpected thing, "Let's get out." It was blazing hot outside. Though I learned all the important areas around the award show area, I still didn't know my way around the rest of the casino, especially when starting out from a random location. The limo doors opened and we were out on the molten sidewalk as the driver pleaded with us to stay. Quickly we scurried into the nearest entrance of the MGM Grand. The last thing we needed was to have her make-up ruined by the heat and I definitely didn't want to be all sweaty for the red carpet pictures. The doors opened and a gust of cold air rushed passed, cooling us off immediately. The minute we stepped into the casino, my eyes scanned the room as my brain raced trying to find something familiar to head towards. At this point, Cyndi said she knew it wasn't my fault as she could see me in stealth mode. She just wanted to get to the carpet ASAP and for me to lead the way. Gulp...

During my five-second pause to try and figure the lay of the land, casino patrons started to notice Cyndi Lauper was in their presence. I mean how couldn't they? She definitely doesn't blend into a crowd. We had to move immediately before we were surrounded, so I started leading them in one direction, hoping a beacon of light would shine and direct me to show. Hanging from the ceiling were plenty of signage-pointing directions to various locations, but none of them were what we needed, or even sounded familiar to me. I had to keep us moving, so I acted as if I knew where we were going and marched on. As we walked, more people actually followed us asking for pictures and shouting out loving comments to Cyndi. It was a cross between a Hallmark moment, because all the love they gave her, and a *Walking Dead* moment, because dozens of people followed us aimlessly. I was the only one there to protect her. I repeatedly told people we had to keep walking and I was sorry she couldn't pose for any pictures at this time. I was sweating more than I would have been outside in the hot Vegas weather.

I frantically tried to radio for help, but no one was responding. The red carpet was in full celebrity arrival mode so they were either wrapped up in what was happening there, or my transmission was not going through because we were too far away. My eyes scanned the room. I prayed I could get her to a safe place soon. I was starting to feel more like a bodyguard getting the president to safety than a celebrity escort.

Then, there was a glimmer of hope. I noticed a place where I had bought a bottle of water the day before. I instantly directed us to the opposite side of the room, where that store was located, hoping I was not confusing it with a similar looking store. To me, casinos are just these huge mazes, with no distinction of where you are so visitors stay inside and spend more money. I kept looking back to Cyndi and her publicist, who were only a few feet behind, to make sure they were all right and not ravaged by the crowd. They seemed wide-eyed and nervous; I just hoped they wouldn't blame me for this adventure from hell, later.

Finally, we reached the store. It was what I had hoped. With any luck, I'd be able to retrace my steps from the day before to find the venue. Once I could get us in that area, I would easily be able to find the red carpet. Luckily, much of the crowd had dwindled away and we only had to worry about any new fans gathering as we approached the venue.

We hopped onto an escalator. While on it, I turned to them to apologize, once again. They told me really not to worry and thanked me for getting them out of there. I don't think they had any idea how lost I really was because I kept that little gem a secret. Once we hit the bottom of the escalator, we had arrived! We were only a few feet now from the red carpet and in the midst of production crewmembers. We did walk the carpet, but the journey getting there was enough excitement for me. I am sure the driver had some explaining to do to his boss later, especially after I made certain my supervisor knew what happened. I certainly was not going to take the blame for this one.

## *67ʰ Annual Golden Globes* 2010 - Beverly Hills, CA

Living in Southern California has many advantages, fine weather at the top of the list. Many mornings my dog Oliver woke me bright and early. I'd stumble out of bed to feed him his breakfast. Half awake, I opened the drapes and peered out the window only to see the same thing; sunny and perfect weather. Yes, some days are a little colder than others, but it is nothing compared to the Northeast I grew up with. When I first moved to Hollywood, I laughed that the meteorologist even had a job because their charts would read something like; Monday 85 degrees, Tuesday 85 degrees, Wednesday 86 degrees, Thursday 87 degrees, etc. Weather wise it's like the movie "Ground Hogs Day!" With that said, there have been some days when the weather was such a star it ruined red carpet arrivals.

It was a gloomy morning and it seemed the powers that be wanted rain to fall. Boy did it. The *Golden Globes* was taking place at the Beverly Hilton where it had been for many years and everything was set up for a glamorous sunny red carpet experience. It rained off and on all morning. By the time afternoon arrived, the sky opened up. It poured in buckets. It was so bad most of us stood under awnings or inside the hotel, rather than escort the celebrities on the carpet. Many celebrities also just wanted to be inside and skipped their anticipated interviews altogether. Reporters seemed miserable hiding under tents and umbrellas anxiously hoping some stars would come speak with them. Luckily, there were a few moments when the rain paused for a few minutes and several celebrities were able to do the soggy walk along the carpet. I remember Sandra Bullock being able to pose in the photo section for a few shots before the rain started to come down again. For everyone though, it was not a pleasant experience.

**Rain is Hollywood's Kryptonite.**
**We never thought it would stop raining!**

One surprising moment was to see Bob Iger (President and Chief Executive Officer of the Walt Disney Company) and his wife trying to make it down the red carpet without an umbrella. I believe, because there was such a shortage of umbrellas, only people who were recognizable super stars received them in hopes to save some of the glamour. Although his face and name may not be recognizable to many people, to me, Bob Iger is a super star. So I snagged an umbrella and rushed it to him just as the sky opened up again. He and his wife gave me the biggest smiles. I imagine it was probably the look he had on his face when he found out he would be running Disney.

Although the red carpet was ruined, and countless guests were soggy, the show went off without a hitch. You can never plan enough, and, even in California, you should keep a few extra umbrellas around.

**Even after all these years, I still love working these shows.**

### *TV Land Awards* 2006 - Los Angeles, CA

I was asked to escort the legendary Donny Osmond. Not only was I *not* a fan, I didn't know much about him at all. Sure, I heard his name thrown around. I knew he sang with his sister and older women nearly fainted at the site of him, but that was about it.

It was the day of the *TV Land Awards*. He was to arrive later in the afternoon so I had an hour or two to wander around the venue and wait. I knew the place like the back of my hand and was well versed on everything I needed to do for the evening. I started to go through the show run down to kill some time, and because I was curious of what other celebrities would be attending that evening. While reading through the list of stars, my heart almost stopped. *His* name was there; his name was really on the list. My all-time favorite actor was going to be there. I had to meet him! I loved this guy for over twenty-five years and with all my time escorting, he had never been at any of the events. He was the guy who had it all. He could sing, dance, act, and have you cracking up. This guy was someone I admired since I was a small child! It was the legendary, Kermit the Frog. Don't laugh, but this cute green frog is the reason I am in show business. Growing up watching him, he shaped my life. Kermit has and always will, hold a special place in my heart.

Knowing he was there to present an award, I had to find him. With an obsessed look in my eyes, I asked several people if they had seen him. Pretty much everyone said no, probably wondering why I was so interested, until my roommate at the time, and fellow celebrity escort Felipe, said he would show me which trailer he was in. Kermit actually had his own freaking trailer! Awesome. We raced to it. Ready to knock on the door I paused, got nervous and paced in front of it a few times. *This is my childhood idol.* I was so nervous. I knew many people feel that way toward Donny Osmond, but mine was a singing frog, that well, wasn't real.

I laughed at myself thinking how ridiculous I was being and remembered the first time I actually saw him in person. Several years earlier, I was walking Oliver down Hollywood Boulevard when I heard a familiar voice. It sounded like Kermit, but what would he be doing on there in the middle of the afternoon. Then I heard it again. Heading toward the voice I went around a corner and saw a crowd of people across the street. *What was going on?* All of a sudden there was an opening in the crowd and I saw Kermit at a podium speaking. Then I realized he was getting his own star on the walk of fame. I laughed to myself, thankful I was not losing my mind. Schoolboy giddiness took over as I watched every movement he made as he spoke to the crowd. Then all of a sudden his head turned and he looked at me! Kermit noticed me. I was so excited that I raised my hand in the air and waived. Mid waive, I realized what I was doing, pulled my hand down and looked around, making sure no one had seen me. *I am waiving at a puppet that doesn't have real eyes.* I was embarrassed, but Kermit made me feel like a kid again. I swear he was looking at me, though.

Outside of Kermit's trailer, I stood and told myself I wouldn't make a fool of myself. I took a deep breath and knocked on the door. I could feel my heart beat in my chest. A middle-aged man answered. As he held the door open halfway, I noticed something green in the background lying on a table. I asked if I could meet Kermit and told him how big a fan I was. At first I thought the guy would think I was nuts, but he simply laughed and told me to wait a minute as he almost fully closed the door.

Seconds later, he opened the door and there was Kermit with him. My heart rate sped up and before I could say a word, another person walked to the door with Miss Piggy. I didn't know what to say-- luckily Felipe had come with me and asked if he could take a picture of us. They agreed and he took several pictures of Kermit and me, and then one with all three. Miss Piggy was a natural, of course, posing and trying to steal the attention from Kermit. She is such a ham! While I was posing, I did make sure to touch Kermit's arm with my fingertips. *I touched Kermit the Frog!* I thought as the picture was capturing this joyful moment.

**Photo Credit: Felipe Piña**

To this day it's one of my favorite pictures. I am happy to share it with you. I didn't want to overstay my welcome, so thanked them and quickly left. It really was great for their handlers to bring them both out for me. It was a moment I will never forget and for that, I thank them.

Later that afternoon Kermit was outside by the private entrance when Diana Ross walked by. Wearing a white fur coat and enormous hair, she froze the moment she saw him. It seemed like it took a second for her to register what she was looking at and she came running over to him. She lit up like a Christmas tree and talked to Kermit as if he was a friend of hers. They may have known each other from other events, but not once did she look at the puppeteer. She kept her eyes focused on Kermit. I realized I am not the only person who is pulled into his world. It was amazing to see Diana Ross star struck on my Kermit--and it made me feel a hell of a lot better that I was as well.

Donny Osmond was incredibly nice that evening, but Kermit stole the spotlight. I did learn a great deal more about Donny and some of the charity work he does. So now I'm an admirer.

## Hand Holding

There have been many touching moments I have been lucky enough to experience while working as a celebrity escort. But when it becomes physically touching it's another type of uniqueness! It always makes me happy when a celebrity literally reaches out and gives me a hug, kiss, or even holds my hand at an event. To me, it means that they are comfortable with me, appreciate the work that I am doing for them and it's a validation by someone who touches people's lives on a massive scale.

A simple hand grab, where a celebrity holds my hand, is special because it connects two people on different life journeys, for a few moments. Yes, it may sound like I am fifteen year old boy writing "so and so held my hand," but each time it happened were unexpected moments I treasured. The whole reason people shake hands in business is to create a personal, deeper connection. So, it would make sense when a certain celebrity actually holds my hand for a while, I feel a deeper connection.

Whether it was from just walking off the red carpet, needing help getting around, or holding my hand to not become separated, it has always been a sweet moment for me. Now the name-dropping of my top three; Betty White, Alyssa Milano and Sophia Loren!

**Betty White:**

I always knew I had a friend growing up because every Saturday night I tuned into, what I still think is one of the best sitcoms in television history, *The Golden Girls*. Betty White's acting ability and humor is unlike any other. Decades later, she is still a fan favorite amongst people of all generations.

I happily accepted the assignment to escort Betty White at the *Teen Choice Awards* in 2010 at the Gibson Amphitheater on the Universal Studios lot in Los Angeles. It is visible en route to the King Kong Attraction during the tram tour of Universal.

Betty and I had been backstage with her longtime assistant when it was time for her to take her seat. We had about twenty minutes before it began, but I did not want us to be rushed. As we headed from backstage to the house, Betty unexpectedly grabbed my hand. I always joke that she was getting frisky, but I truly felt as if I was holding my grandmother's hand and it put me in a sense of pure ease. It made me actually think of my grandmothers, in that moment, and how lucky I was to have them for so long in my life. I also had a flash of me as a boy on my parent's bed watching *The Golden Girls* and laughing my head off at the jokes I didn't understand at the time.

**Photo Credit: John Gabaldon**

As we continued to hold hands, we walked through the doorway that led us into the house. We were about ten steps in and the audience noise changed from loud and talking to a weird mumble. I could feel the excitement as thousands of people watched our every step. Just as we got maybe twenty feet further, the entire audience stood and started to clap. People began to cheer and shout, "I love you" and Betty stopped to look around. She seemed a little confused as if she was missing something going on around her. I quickly realized what had happened so I leaned over and told her the standing ovation was for her. Betty was stunned and told me, "I don't believe it." We took a few more steps and stopped again. She looked out and waved to everyone. Then she peered up at me and said, "I wasn't even going to come. I didn't think kids even knew who I am." She waved to everyone as they continued to clap until we reached her seat. *Never* have I *ever* experienced an audience's reaction like this. It was a shocking and beautiful moment.

**Betty and I during rehearsals of the *Daytime Emmys***

There were three open seats at the time so I sat with her and her assistant until the start of the show. I mentioned to Betty my ninety-two year old grandmother called Betty 'just a kid' (Betty was eighty-nine at the time). She laughed saying maybe she should get some advice from an older gal like her. Jimmy Fallon was sitting a section over and came over to say hello to her. He was very kind and introduced himself to her assistant and me. Many times people ignore everyone the star is with; it's nice when you have someone so respectful. Betty and I spoke about her upcoming projects and how her popularity just shot up again unexpectedly. I felt like the star that evening because I was lucky enough to hold this legend's hand. She was what I always imagined her to be. No wonder why America loves Betty White!

**Alyssa Milano:**

Alyssa wanted me to be the boss when I escorted her to the *Unicef Benefit* in 2007. This heavily tattooed vixen was attending with a very tall boyfriend at the time. He seemed new to the red carpet world, yet he was very chill and soaking it all in. We walked down the red carpet and finished with press. All three of us headed into the ballroom of the Beverly Hilton Hotel when she reached out and grabbed my hand. It was definitely a nice friendship grab, but it made me a little nervous because her boyfriend was standing right behind me. He didn't seem bothered, but you can never be too careful. I wondered why she was not holding his hand. I walked with her hand in hand to their table as other celebrity escorts stared at me with jealousy. I did not want to become a punching bag for her boyfriend, but it's not every day a beautiful woman wants to hold my hand so when one does, who am I to say no?

**Sophia Loren:**

This legendary Italian actress is not only a classic beauty, but winner of an *Academy Award*, *Golden Globe* and even a *Grammy* (just to mention a few)! I was at the *Golden Globes* in 2010 where it was my responsibility to bring specific celebrities backstage before they were to present an award. Sophia was not one of my responsibilities, but someone from the talent department, on the spur of the moment, asked if I would bring her backstage. I quickly jumped at the opportunity and we were introduced. She definitely had aged since her most famous roles in the 1950's, 1960's, and 1970's, but still looked stunning. She seemed very grateful to have me escort her and held my hand as we walked backstage before she was to present the award to someone for the Best Foreign Film. Industry professionals all watched us instead of what was currently happening on stage as we brushed by their seats to the side of the room. I sadly had not watched anything she had done so I couldn't be a fan, but I definitely respected her place in the entertainment world. She had not attended any of the shows that I was at over the previous ten years so I knew this appearance was a real treat. I actually felt as if I was with the Queen of England as we walked backstage. Immediately after she presented, I called my father (whose parents are from Italy) because I knew he would appreciate who I had just met, just like any red blooded American who grew up watching that bombshell.

## *VH1 Divas: A Tribute to Diana Ross* 2000 - New York City

The world survived Y2K and it was April 2000. I was assigned to escort LaDonna Adrian Gaines--better known as Grammy award winning disco diva Donna Summer. I was excited for this opportunity since there were many nights I popped in her CD while driving to the clubs in Washington, D.C. I only had "discovered" her in 1997, but you could say I was very familiar with her music three years later. That lady knew how to belt some notes! When I first met her, I had to remind myself to not smile too much. It's always said, "never meet any of your idols, for they will disappoint you." Well I was thankful Donna did not do that, she was very humble and ready from the moment she arrived to do what was necessary to put on a good show.

During rehearsals, the day before the show, I was told by production there was some backstage drama between Mariah Carey and Diana Ross. Donna and I sat and waited in her dressing room for hours while being told very little about what was happening. I heard, at one point, those divas didn't show up to rehearse the Supremes' medley--all three of them were supposed to sing together. Donna Summer was very unhappy about this because she wanted to rehearse the song as a group. We never seemed to get a clear answer on what really happened so Donna rehearsed her solo song and then left angry.

The next day during the show, Mariah Carey and Diana Ross sang the medley together without Donna. Donna told me she was so angry about them skipping the rehearsal and wasting her time, she refused to do it with them. She did not want to give people an unrehearsed show and felt very disrespected since Diana Ross, herself, asked Donna to be a part of the show in the first place. Instead, Donna sang two solo songs of her own, which were incredible. Although Donna was angry, she never took it out on me or anyone else. She actually seemed sad rather than anything else.

**Me and Donna Summer**

At one point in the evening, from the audience, emerged an extremely excited woman asking if I worked for Donna Summer. She said she had seen me with her throughout the evening and hoped Donna and I were close. She practically begged me to see if she could meet Donna and speak with her. Obviously, I couldn't bring some over eager fan back to meet with Donna. Not only was it a security risk, but also just weird. As I was explaining to the woman I was only her escort and didn't know Donna personally, I realized the worked up fan was actress Hillary Swank! She said she grew up listening to all of Donna's songs and had always dreamt of meeting her. Eager to please, I brought

Hillary and her then husband, Chad Lowe, backstage and made the introduction. Hillary was so grateful she thanked me several times that evening and waved anytime I walked by her seat. It was my pleasure doing this favor because not only was Hillary a sweet heart, but she is a very talented actress. It just shows another case for the fact that celebrities are fans of other celebrities, too!

I was very saddened by the news of Donna Summer's death in May 2012. I reflected back on the brief days and moments we shared and how humble she was. I also wondered what Hillary was thinking when she heard the news and if they ever stayed in touch. Donna Summer was referenced as a Diva, but to me she was a woman with many great talents, a big heart, and a whole lot of hit songs.

# YOU ARE WHAT YOU WEAR

Most celebrities tend to look glamorous at every event. *Is that natural? How can I look that good? Do they feel as good as they look?* These are some of the questions asked when watching a red-carpeted event. Everyone knows many celebrities have a team of people helping them look their best, even so, fashion disasters occur, yet most of the time they look amazing. With a team of experts and money, celebrities can flaunt their assets, but how is an average celebrity escort supposed to fit in? We hardly make any money as it is, how could we afford to dress like the stars? Yet we are expected to look just as good as them on the red carpet.

We all have had that struggle to look and feel our best. But try figuring out what to wear to the *Grammy Awards*, with little to no money and the possibility of appearing on millions of television screens worldwide. It's a bit more daunting than planning for a company Christmas party. Obviously, the party is important, but imagine hearing that in a week you will be going to a major award show where cameras will be pointed on you from every direction. Sure, it may seem easy for a *guy* to dress up, and I do have to admit I have far fewer options to choose from, and playing dress up and fashion were never been my things. Some days I was lucky to have matching socks. The only time I looked at a label was to see the price.

In addition to my barbaric fashion mentality, every award show has a different style requirement and an escorted celebrity with their own trend setting expectations. To complicate things further, many times, I don't meet the celebrity until the day of the event. This leaves no time to decide what to wear to complement their look for the evening. Celebrities are not expecting me to wow them, but I still feel the need to blend in.

A few shows provide a tuxedo for the escorts. An escort emails their measurements and their tux will be at the venue for pick up the day of the event.

Unlike many celebrity escorts, I want to go the extra mile and figure out what clothing or colors would match the celebrity's style, or personality, and of course make me look my best. I feel enhancing their style puts them more at ease from the start and creates the best possible working relationship. Maybe I'm making too much of it, but in part it's because I desire to look like I belong on their arm versus some awkward guy standing next to Hollywood's finest. Therefore, every event is a struggle in what to wear.

I wore silver pants (yes silver, ugh) at the *VH1 Vogue Fashion Awards* in 1999 while escorting Sharon Stone. I thought she would appreciate the flashy fun feel. But, when I was with Tom Hanks at the *GQ Men of the Year Awards* that same year, I wore a classic black tuxedo. These are two completely different looks for two different celebrities and situations. Yes, the silver pants were a bit much, but at the time I thought they were stunning and sheik for an enormous fashion event.

On a normal day, I don't put much thought into what I wear. I am a typical guy who loves to wear a t-shirt and jeans. In fact, in middle school I think I wore sweat pants for all of eighth grade. So when I first began escorting, I had very little acceptable clothing options to choose from. I also was living in one of the most expensive cities in the world, shopping was a challenge and a necessity. I was not trying to keep up with the Jones'; I was trying to keep up with the Kardasians!

In the early years of escorting, I pounded the pavement going into store after store to search for something cool yet affordable. The cheaply made club clothing I owned only went so far. I also felt I couldn't wear the same thing over and over again, because I was sure celebrities and crewmembers would notice and realize I didn't belong. I didn't want to lose this awesome opportunity, in which I was quickly excelling. I was determined to be the best celebrity escort in the world and was convinced that dressing well was going to help get me there.

## Celebrity Escort: Fashion Thief?

With all of this added self-pressure, I have a confession to make. No, I have not murdered anyone for flashy threads, but I did do something that many may be guilty of (or maybe I'm just saying that to alleviate my own guilt). Although I never outright stole anything, I did buy a few items, wore them to events and then returned them the following day. Now I know the police are not going to arrive at my door as I type this, but this is not the best way to go through life. I wanted to have my cake and eat it too--with a stylish fork, of course. Being a poor kid in New York City trying to fit in with celebrities, I figured it was only a tiny crime to comment.

When I did the *VH1 Vogue Fashion Awards* in 2000 I had been escorting for a year and it was the second time I worked that particular show. This event requires a fun, hip, and sexy outfit, so the tux I wound up buying needed to stay hanging in the closet. My rent at the time was only $600 a month including utilities. And it was rumored Sandra Bullock was moving into a place two blocks away! (I had been very lucky because I scored a rent-controlled apartment in the hip SoHo neighborhood of Manhattan.) Everything was going well and amazingly, bills were being paid, but there was nothing left over for clothing. Even buying new shoelaces would have thrown me in the red.

Two nights before the event, I frantically searched through my closet to see what I could mix and match to create an outfit. There was nothing I had not worn already several times. Desperation occurred so the next day I decided I had to go shopping. Everything I wanted either didn't fit right or was too expensive. I had no time to waste. I searched store after store. I just needed something I could feel good about. After four hours of looking at a dizzy array of eye numbing garments, I found one of the sexiest jackets I had ever seen. Maybe it was my body shutting down due to an overload of fashion, but there it was, a brown leather jacket that felt like silk when I touched it.

It was several hundred dollars, but seemed to be worth every penny. I tried it on partly hoping it would look terrible, but instead it felt like a glove lined with feathers. I couldn't resist its sleekness so it was then when I came up with the sinister plan. I would buy it, but I was only going to wear it for a few hours and then return it the next day. My plan was in place and I was signing the credit card slip before I knew it. When I arrived home, I instantly taped the tags into the sleeves of the jacket and hung it on a hanger in the living room so I would just need to slip it over my old mix match clothing before heading to the show the next day. No one would care about my other clothes because the jacket was the scene-stealer.

While at the show, I spent the entire evening strutting around in the jacket and showing off my sexy self. I swear this jacket opened doors for me and I was able to have conversations with just about everyone. This jacket was magic and at one point someone asked if I wanted to sit in the audience and said I "look like a celebrity." Since my talent had left for the evening, I jumped at the opportunity and got an incredible seat for the remaining part of the show.

Gisele Bundchen and Cuba Gooding Jr. were the hosts and celebrity after celebrity appeared on the stage just a few feet in front of me. This was my first time ever sitting in the audience, and although I had been seeing celebrities backstage while I was working, it was exciting to see them up close from a comfortable seat.

I remember feeling so amazed and wide eyed when out of the corner of my eyes I saw something shiny to my left. I looked over and noticed a woman two seats away with the most incredible legs I have ever seen! They were perfect and glimmered in the light. My eyes followed her glorious curves up further along this twinkling path to her shorts/skirt skimpy outfit when I quickly realized they belonged to Jennifer Lopez. *WOW*, I thought. I was sitting two seats away from Jennifer Lopez. She was this relatively new sexy Latina breakout star with catchy stimulating music. She looked fresh and flawless. I quickly looked away as I didn't want her to notice I was staring.

Maybe I was just drunk from celebrity overdrive, but I wondered how her legs were so sexy. I began to study them once again. They looked so damn perfect. As I looked closer, I could have sworn they were covered in make-up! Is that the secret I thought? Women all over the world will see her in pictures and on camera and her legs will be glowing sexy because they are coated with make-up? I thought this was interesting and if true, why don't they make a commercial make-up for women's legs? It was genius! I know genetics, working out, and eating well helped make her legs incredible, but I am sure it was the make-up that helped to create the most incredible legs I have ever seen. I just hoped she noticed my sexy jacket.

The next day, I returned the jacket and got a full refund. It was difficult because it seemed like my new lucky jacket created opportunities. And some people even thought I was a celebrity, that's how good it looked. It even allowed me to open up and speak to some people I would have normally shied away from. I had to return it though, because I was broke and knew there would be once again another show where I needed something *else* to wear. I had succeeded with my plan--but had I really? Looking back no one was harmed, but I did pretend I was something I was not. It gave me this false confidence and made me start to value my looks over my talent and personality. It obviously wasn't a magical jacket, but it allowed me to come out of my shell and be more myself, causing me to have a great evening.

## How Do I Look?

Let's face it; celebrities have enormous amounts of the pressure to look their best at these events because their careers and livelihoods can depend on it. They are scrutinized, from their hair down to the color of their lipstick. They feel they have to hire a team of people to help make them look flawless. In fact, a make-up artist alone can charge up to $10,000 per day (I should have gotten into make-up). Regardless, celebrities sometimes blindly follow guidance and advice from people who only want to suck up to them. I have had countless times at award shows when some sexy vixen asks me which dress she should wear or how does she look. It's not a flippant question, but one where I felt her self-value would crumble with a badly phrased sentenced on my part. I think it's because deep down, she knows something is not right.

I try to be a very honest person, so if I don't like the dress, I say so. This shocks many of the underlings that swarm the celebrities and kiss their ass. I have seen many people give terrible advice to celebrities just so they don't upset them and in hopes they will get hired again. Everything is always SO great and everything is SO wonderful all the time! That is not how I roll. I will be polite and respectful, but if someone looks terrible in a dress I will tell her. The only exception to this rule is if the celebrity asks me minutes or even seconds before she is to appear on stage. If I gave a truthful answer at that point, it would serve no good. The celebrity would just be even more nervous and mess up her presentation or speech. After being put in this awkward situation once, I choose to always tell a white lie, but only when necessary.

I am not sure how, soothing celebrities and making them even laugh during the most stressful moments are a few of my strengths. I truly care about each individual I work with and try to see things from their perspective. I also think my honest opinions are appreciated. They tend to trust me and relax in my presence, especially if we have worked together before.

One of these occasions I escorted Kirstie Alley at the *TV Land Awards* in 2007. I must say Kirstie is full of life. Her energy level was through the roof; however, her nerves were as well. She seemed to be a nervous wreck. I tried to reassure her.

While waiting backstage to present an award to Lucie Arnaz and Desi Arnaz Jr. in honor of their mother Lucille Ball, Kirstie was fidgeting and adjusting her dress obsessively. She asked me if she looked fat in the dress and if she looked good overall. I took a critical look at her and thought she looked decent, but I honestly didn't think the dress was as good as she deserved. It looked very simple; she should have a more vivacious look. Keep in mind, I know nothing about fashion, however, she did ask my opinion. Kirstie was about twenty seconds away from going on to present the award. I had to lie to her. I told her she looked fantastic and she would be awesome. If it had been thirty minutes earlier I would have asked to see what other options she had to wear.

I think Kirstie can be very sexy, but because of her weight battles it has made her insecure. This is sad, because when confident, she is very sexy no matter what her weight is. She did do a great job and I am sure all of America thought she looked great. But I still think she deserved a better look. I still feel bad for lying to her and almost told her years later when I saw her, again.

One of the reasons I tell this story is because in households across the world, women ask their husbands, "How do I look in this?" If he is a good guy he will be honest and should be appreciated. But, at the doorstep of the house for a dinner party and he says anything less than "You are stunning," then he is a fool! I realized *all* people can be insecure. Many times celebrities are put in this magic bubble, but they feel insecurity just like all of us.

## Image in Hollywood

The entertainment industry somehow knows how to get under your skin and emphasize all personal insecurities. The pressure to stay in good shape, be well groomed, and look my best sometimes feels overwhelming. I know I'm not a model. I know the attention was on the celebrity and not me, yet I still feel, especially when first starting out, that I needed to look the part.

Much of this pressure is unspoken and probably in my head, but I think many people suffer from this whether they work in entertainment or not. I use the word suffer because I think of it as a sort of illness. Each day what I reflected back in the mirror determined whether it was going to be a good day or not. If I didn't like my image, I got upset, frustrated, and even angry. I never had this problem before I worked in the industry.

In a way, I have become my own enemy--a mini monster that forgets what really is important. I definitely don't think of myself as shallow and tend not to judge what other people look like. Yet with myself, I have this odd, warped, critical laser focused vision that critiques myself so hard I don't want to get out of bed. Sadly, it seems I have caught this from living in the city of beauty and movie stars.

Yet I am the one to blame. This added weight on my soul, holding me back from being who I am and who I am meant to be. It's like a constant inner civil war that rages within me; one side critiquing and putting me down, the other trying to have confidence and courage. Here is one story of how my vanity backfired.

In order to look and feel my best I thought a nice tan would help. Just as there are numerous ways for women to look better, I quickly learned there are for men. Some things I tried, some things I continue to do, and some things I have avoided--well at least so far.

Many times I would go to a tanning booth before a show so I would have that nice glow. Even in the later years I did this. In 2010, a day before the *American Music Awards*, I decided to get a fake-n-bake tan so I would look good and natural next to Jenny McCarthy. To me Jenny was the perfect person to escort. I knew she would be fun and not take everything seriously. I had not fake tanned in years, so I was excited to have a nice glow. Sadly, I misjudged how long my skin could tolerate the rays. The day of the show, a day after the tan, I was beet red. Although it did not hurt, I could feel the heat flowing from my skin and looked as if I could guide Santa's sleigh through any storm. I tried everything from a cold shower to putting on make-up to tone it down, but nothing worked. I looked like a fool. I was so embarrassed I almost stayed home.

**Jenny McCarthy and I Excited for the Show**

Trying to look my best turned me into a sideshow freak. When I met Jenny, luckily she never said anything. In fact, she was extremely cool and I mentioned I was writing this book. She told me she wanted to be in it, so here you are Jenny! She also asked to take some pictures with me to include. Here we are together at the Nokia Theatre in downtown Los Angeles after walking the red carpet. Because it is a black and white picture in the printed book, you can't really see my glow, but if you go to www.armcandybook.com, or are reading this online, you will see me in all my red glory!

Luckily, as the years went by I felt more secure because I knew I was good at my job. I learned to stop being so critical about myself. I also learned we need to stop comparing ourselves to others and stop judging ourselves so harshly. I have thankfully never done anything drastic to lose weight or change the way I look. But I have ruined precious moments of my life criticizing myself and being cruel to myself with horrible thoughts. I have to make a conscious effort to remember health is the most important thing.

I know people who will spend money on Botox and treatments, yet they don't have health insurance. This is all insane behavior and we all need to stop. No one is perfect and striving to be perfect is a waste of time. In fact, the best things in life are not perfect. My favorite t-shirt has a rip in it. My favorite photos of myself are when they were taken and I didn't know or when I'm not worried about how I look. If we were able to become perfect, how boring would that be?

After becoming an expert and feeling confident in my abilities and secure enough in my looks, I heard from a few staff members that I was getting too old to be an Escort. This was crazy. I was in my early thirties. But if this was a possibility, even if just one person thought it, I now had a new set of worries to think about. I suddenly knew how many women must feel in this crazy industry. Luckily, I learned to ignore negative people by then, so this did not really rattle me. Hopefully my battle against this physically self-loathing is over and I have found a health balance once again.

Through these years I have learned quite a bit about fashion, grooming and about looking your best. Here are some tips I learned from the biggest stars and the best make-up, hair and wardrobe stylist.

## How to Look Your Best at Any Event

1) Be you! I am sure you heard it before, but it's true. Nothing is sexier than seeing a guy or a girl confident about themselves. Your quirkiness or uniqueness should be appreciated and celebrated. Your sense of style is who you are, so wear what you like and what best represents you. Embrace it, just make sure it is appropriate for the event you are going to attend or you will get the wrong type of attention. You may look hot in that mini skirt, but wearing it to your bosses' cocktail party is a terrible move. If you are unsure of the attire for an event, just ask!

2) Expensive doesn't mean good. We always hear this celebrity wore this name at this event. Did you know that most times the clothing is loaned or given to the celebrity? They didn't spend $5,000 for a dress, even though they may be able to afford it, so why would you buy something you can't afford? Buy only what you can afford comfortably. You can't really smile and be happy when you know you are wearing something that is not true to you, or so expensive you are terrified on how you are going to pay the credit card bill.

3) Prepare ahead. Buy or prepare outfits at least a week before the event. Having the pressure of making a last minute decision does not make the choice better or easier. You also can have the opportunity to look for

good sales or deals when you have time. Often you can find the same item of clothing cheaper somewhere else, if you just look.

4) Black is over used. Some black is good, it is slimming after all, but use is sparingly. Add some color or interesting patterns to liven you up. Everyone starts looking like fashion zombies and identical. This is your chance to sparkle and show yourself to the people at the event. Why blend in?

5) Go easy on the make-up. Stop hiding yourself! A little make-up goes a long way. You don't need to look like a drag queen or clown. Make-up is supposed to enhance your beauty and cover up your defects; not change you into another person. For men, I see nothing wrong with a little powder or covering up pimples, but it needs to be very subtle. If someone can tell you are wearing make-up you may get the title of Boy George.

6) Know your body type and dress accordingly. Many people think they can wear whatever they want whenever they want. Of course they can, but it doesn't mean they will look good in it or it will be appropriate! You should look sexy, but when it is pushed too far, you may get confused with being a whore and nobody respects that.

7) Don't have unrealistic expectations. You are who you are, right now. If you are twenty pounds overweight, then so be it. Wearing a tight shirt or dress only amplifies your fat more. Wear something that fits and is appropriate to the event. If you have to buy the next size up, do it.

There is nothing you can do at that moment. But, the next day just hit the gym and continue to so the next event you can wear what you want. I have learned that lesson first hand, as my love handles took over one party where I knew everyone noticed. It was embarrassing. Not because I had gained a few pounds, but because I actually wore something that made me look worse, instead of dealing with my own reality.

8) Being comfortable is important in what you wear. If it's not comfortable, you will not look comfortable. This builds on number seven but also refers to things like shoes. You may look great for the first hour, but if you are carrying your shoes around for the rest of the evening, you come across as annoying and high maintenance.

9) I am a huge fan of personal grooming. Just maintain all body hair so it's manageable. Men can get their eyebrows waxed as well. It is an upkeep that can be annoying because you have to run back to the place every two or three weeks, but can really open up your face. To be very honest, I don't know how women do it so easily. Every time I have had my eyebrows waxed it felt like torture and I am red for two days. It is the worst pain I have felt in my life! Just make sure you do it a few days before the event because your skin will be irritated for several days.

10) Don't spend too much on hair. I go to Supercuts and get a great haircut for $16. Some of my friends spend upwards to $60 on a men's haircut. If you get a good hairdresser, no matter where you go, it is worth it. Save that money though and find someone good that is

affordable. I often get compliments on my hair and it's all thanks to Supercuts and some quick styling on my part.

11) If you are going to be on television or recorded on any video device, there are certain clothing guidelines you should follow. Never wear white. It will not only make you look heavier, but if you have Caucasian skin it will make you look paler. White also reflects the light making everything less flattering. Never wear crazy patterns or stripes. This tends to look fluttered or strobe on camera. Avoid shiny jewelry because as you may have guessed, they shine into the camera and are distracting. Remember, just because you look good in person does not mean it will translate on camera. Keep these rules in mind if you are going to an event being recorded.

Now that you look great, don't ruin it by looking bad in the photos. I have ruined many, many, many photos because I was posing wrong and now those photos will haunt me in social media forever.

## How to Look Like a Celebrity in Photos

Why do so many celebrities look good on red carpets? Is it because of the extraordinary abilities? Maybe, but people tend to forget they do have make-up artists and hair stylists doing touch ups moments before they arrive on the carpet. You may not have access to these amenities, but posing for a picture is very important. There are some ways to help make you look good for any photos you are taking. Here are a few tips I've learned over the years...

1) Don't get nervous! Many people, including me, hate still photographs so they become nervous. Nerves make you freeze up and can create an awkward pose that will make you look less attractive in the picture. If it's a friend, try to have them catch you off guard.

2) Relax, smile, and let your inner beauty shine through. It sounds like crap, but I it helps. Also, a stiff drink always helps me. If I am at an event I'll wait to take photos until after I've had one. If I wait too long though, I may have missed my opportunity because I'm a lightweight.

3) This may sound silly, but practice in front of a camera. Try different angles, smiles, clothing options etc. Once you know what works for you you're golden.

4) Try to make sure the camera is always a little above you. When you shoot any person, angled up, it makes them look less attractive. That's what they do in horror movies so unless you want to look like Frankenstein, insist they either angle the camera down, or get a tall person to take the picture. On red carpets, the photographers are almost always on a stage, platform, stool, or something higher than the celebrities for this reason.

5) Lean into the camera. Face First! Most people get shy or nervous and tend to pull back. This will give you a double chin or at the very least make you look like your head is attached directly to your chest. It is a hard habit to break, but keep doing it until you naturally are able to without thinking about it.

6) Shoulders back, chest out, turn your body so they shoot more of an angle of you, and make sure you hold your head high so your neck is not squished up. Now, this sounds like a workout out, but if you practice a bunch of times it will become more natural.

7) Stand straight and tall, but bend one leg forward. Standing with both legs together make you look weak and unstable. Be confident with your stand!

8) Remember, these celebrities have been doing it for years so never compare yourself to a professional. Just work on your own poses and you will be great!

9) Remember rule number two and just have fun. There is a delete button on those cameras so if it is terrible, in most cases you can erase. If your photo is taken by paparazzi, even if they do use it, people will forget about it a few days later...let's hope.

**Working the Red Carpet of the *Primetime Emmys***
**Photo Credit: Adam Oko**

# JULIA

I literally was shaking in my forty dollar, polished dress shoes after hearing Julia Robert's voice become serious and directed at me. Having the Queen of Hollywood disappointed or upset carries a heavy weight. Whatever someone wants, whether they are a celebrity, producer or director, people tend to scramble and lose all sense of self to get it. I have seen people literally trip over their own feet trying to make themselves look skilled enough to be in the presence of the Hollywood elite. Most people who survive the shark-infested waters of Hollywood cower and give in under this sort of pressure, no matter who the celebrity is, yet here I was with one of the biggest stars. Of course, bowing to their needs may be the smart thing to do, but in this case, I chose not to.

It was October 2000 and I was assigned to escort the lovely, talented, and outspoken Susan Sarandon. I admired this woman of strength. However, my mother, who enjoyed her as an actress, thought she was a 'troublemaker' because of her willingness to publicly share her political beliefs. The show had begun and we were backstage talking and waiting for Susan's moment to present an award to Elton John when this bubbly woman with slick, dark shoulder length hair walked in. It was Julia Roberts and she looked stunning even without her big curly *Pretty Woman* hair. Julia was not someone I had worked with at yet in my very early career, nor was she someone I was working with that evening. This was the first time I had ever seen her in person and now she was just across the room from me. Having loved every movie she had starred in (well not *Hook*), it was one of those moments when I had to not act like a crazy fan and scream, "I love you!" For me, she is the picture perfect image of the words, *Movie Star.*

Julia strutted over and headed in my direction. My thoughts were stuck in park while my body felt frozen and unable to move. Just as she was a few feet from me, she turned and gave Susan a hug. For a brief stupid moment I thought she was coming over to say hello to me! Actually, a huge relief came over me because I had no idea what I would have said to her. They started chatting away and I stood there like a third wheel listening to the entire conversation. I went from excited, to relief, to feeling sad I was left out. I had just met Susan so why would she introduce me to a big star, especially since I was there working? It took a few minutes to realize, but then I recalled they worked on the film *Step Mom* together, which is why they were so chummy. I did enjoy that movie, and yes I have to admit I shed some tears having had my own mother battle Cancer twice. As I reminisced about this, I tried not to listen to their conversation any further, but it was difficult not to. Besides, I had to be there to make sure I was attending to Susan's needs, so what else was I to do?

Suddenly, Julia turned and looked right at me. *Oh my God, Julia Roberts is looking at me!* I thought. Her eyes locked on mine and I felt as if my insides started to melt. I was like a cartoon dog in love that floats off the ground and high into the air. I have seen her in movies for many years, loved everything she had done, but she had no idea *I* even existed in the world until that moment. As I pictured my own romantic comedy starting with some funny banter, she simply told me she needed to be on stage at that moment to present an award.

Snapping out of my little fantasy, I quickly pulled out the schedule I had tucked into my tuxedo coat's inside pocket and flipped through the pages searching for where she was listed. Seconds seemed like hours, but soon enough I found her scheduled time on stage and told her she still had about twenty-two minutes before she would be on. As she rebutted, her voice raised an octave or two and told me I "must be mistaken" and she was expected to go on now.

Before people go on stage they can become a little nervous (I'd probably vomit a few times), but her inflection was forceful and it scared me. I shuffled through my papers to make sure I was not missing anything. Nope, I was correct and so I explained again to Julia she would be on in about twenty minutes and I would give her a five-minute warning if she wished. Assisting Julia was not my responsibility, but being she is one of my favorite actresses, I figured why not help since she either didn't have an escort, or the one she had was completely worthless. She once again strongly insisted she needed to be presenting within the next minute or so as she had been instructed previously, and was going to miss her cue if we didn't move now. I looked at the nearby monitor and noticed Ben Affleck speaking on stage. According to my paper work, I was definitely right in my assessment, but I became so nervous that I stared down at her shoes like a schoolboy in the principal's office. Everything blurred. She could have been wearing bunny slippers for all I remember, but I knew I was right and didn't want her to make a mistake by going on stage at the wrong time.

I gathered up my courage. This time my voice was firm and I said, "I am sorry, but you are wrong. I have the schedule and I know when you should be on. You arrived a few minutes late and several things changed during that time that you probably are not aware of. I am sorry if you were misinformed." All of a sudden there was silence--a deafening silence. Right then, I realized I was arguing with Julia Roberts and I told her she was wrong! You just don't do that in Tinsletown. Someone overhearing this could have me thrown out. I was *not* trying to upset her, but help her, however, that's probably not how it would look to anyone finding out about this later. I knew my best interest was for her at all times so I felt fine with my statement and firmness. I grew up learning to speak my mind and to be as open and honest as I could with people. Sadly, in Hollywood, it just doesn't happen often enough.

After taking my stance, Julia simply said three words and it changed my life forever. Her words were, "Oh, thank you." In that moment I realized I *needed* to trust myself. It was an odd feeling because I hate to create waves, but I knew I was right and didn't want her to make a fool of herself. If I had just nodded to her and let her go on, hopefully, a stage manager would have stopped her. But you never know, she could have walked out there.

At the end of the evening, I was standing outside making sure various celebrities where getting back into their limos with ease when I noticed Julia leaving with her then boyfriend Benjamin Bratt. Julia waved goodbye to the transportation crew and then noticed me. *Oh no*, I thought. She is going to point me out to someone and complain. I just wanted to do a good job and telling the truth was going to be the end of me. We were at least forty feet apart and she looked right into my eyes and mouthed the words "Thank you". She then waved and ducked into her limo. I felt like I was in the sweet ending to one of her movies. I stood there shocked and elated. So many things raced through my mind, including (for some odd reason) the line "Cindefuckingrella".

This is what I think may have happened. She probably has worked with a lot of incompetent people who cower because she is famous. When I had a backbone and was firm with my answers she respected me more because I owned my job. She realized I was a professional and on top of everything so she didn't need to worry. At the time though, I felt hurt and scared. Even though it ended well, I was bothered by our disagreement.

Why wouldn't I have stood my ground? I think most people go through life not paying attention to their work or not wanting to be responsible for decisions. Even though my job was very small in the scheme of life, I owned it. I believe she respected me more because of that and most importantly, I respected myself. It reminded me of the lesson I learned from my grandmother to stand up for myself and be confident (but not cocky).

Almost a decade later, I was asked to work a benefit in San Francisco and to escort Julia Roberts to the event. I jumped at the chance! These charity shows are always great events to work because for the most part, the celebrities *really* want to be there and believe in the cause. In addition, the crews tend to be smaller and everyone is extra nice because they know their time is spent on a worthwhile cause.

I felt like a minor celebrity when the organization paid for my flight and put me up in a rather nice hotel. I even had car service available to me if I wanted it. Typically on shows, I just drive from my home to the venue, but this was in San Francisco and we all were treated well. There were two days I needed to work with Julia and I couldn't wait to see her again after all these years (this was the first time I would have even seen her since that day in 2000). While I had done dozens of award shows since then, I never ran into her.

An hour before she was to arrive at the venue, I met with one of her security guards who turned out to be a friendly man. I gave him a quick tour of the venue and we put together our plan for the day. We exchanged cell phone numbers. He worked for Julia for many years and adored her. You can tell a lot about a celebrity by the security people they have. When someone works for a star loves them, you know the star treats them well. More often than not, I meet miserable assistants or security personal, which always clues me in to be careful.

Later that day, when Julia arrived sporting a pair of jeans, I introduced myself and brought her backstage to meet the producers of the event. She did not seem to remember me from our short encounter eight years prior. This event was for children with disabilities and she was set to give a speech. She arrived a little earlier than needed, thirty minutes before she was schedule to rehearse. So we just chatted.

Everything was going well and I was enjoying our conversation when the voice in my head took over, telling me to bring up our last encounter. I really wanted to see if she had remembered. It had been so many years, and probably a tiny, forgettable matter to her, but to me, it was a big moment in my life. The curiosity really was overwhelming so I took a deep breath, turned to her, and said the embarrassing words "Do you remember me from a few years ago? You yelled at me backstage." Julia seemed shocked and looked at me as if she thought I was joking.

She asked, "I yelled at you?" I stated, "Yes".

Realizing I was serious, she asked what she yelled about, as she didn't recall anything. Julia also followed up by saying that if she did yell at me, she was very sorry. I could tell she meant it and it was not said just to move on with the awkward moment I created. I explained the situation in detail and thankfully we both ended up laughing. I felt a little foolish because looking back it was no big deal, but as a new escort in 2000 it was very upsetting to me. As people, we tend to hold onto some memories, feel bad about things, don't talk to people we should, or waste life worrying about situations others don't even blink at.

That day I realized how amazing Julia Roberts truly is. She took that conversation and decided to playfully pick on me as if we were siblings. For the next two days she would call me "her handler." She would shout out "where's my handler? I need my handler and you need to be standing next to me not across the room." It was funny and people took her seriously at first, thinking she was upset, but most people saw her beautiful joking smile after she made those comments. I joked back comments such as telling her to go find him because I quit.

After Julia finished her rehearsal, there was some time before the show, so she decided to go to her hotel room and relax. I decided to use this time to search the streets of San Francisco to find what I thought would be the perfect gift for her. I wanted to give her a bell to ring if she needed my help. I was looking for the type of bell used on television shows when someone is sick and they ring it constantly to annoy the person taking care of them. Of course it was a joke gift, but I thought she would get a kick out of it. I put my sneakers to pavement and walked down numerous blocks, but to no avail. I started to question storeowners and even people on the street, but no one knew where I could buy a simple bell. After a frustrating hour, I decided I too needed a break and went back to my hotel room to relax. The idea of it still makes me chuckle. Damn, San Fran and their lack of bells!

The event wound up being a huge success and I have many cherished memories from that weekend including seeing Julia's compassion for the children. Often celebrities will go onstage, do their little speech and leave. Instead of sneaking out the back door, Julia insisted I bring her to where the children with disabilities were gathered--a sort of green room for them to relax and watch the show on a monitor. She took the time to talk to *every single* one of them. The kids took pictures with her and she spent a great deal of time with them. This was done without media and without cameras capturing it for press. She did it because she wanted to, and for no other reason. She IS the ultimate movie star.

Since then, when I have seen her out at award shows, she has always says hello to me and even gives me a hug. In fact, at the *2009 Golden Globes*, Julia walked around holding my hand! We were in the ballroom. I was getting her to her seat and later bringing her backstage when, she comfortably held my hand. It raised a lot of eyebrows. "Who is that with Julia?" I could hear many studio executives mumbling as we passed by their tables. I felt like a prince because people who normally ignored me wondered why I was so special.

I have grown and come a long way because of Julia Roberts. To this day, I try to do what is right, not just what is easy in life. I stand up for what I believe in. Most importantly, I stand up for myself. Many people have this same demon in their own lives--afraid to be themselves.

I understand this fear, but we are all individuals who need to nourish our quirks and be confident that we are not perfect. No one is! I hope this book helps you to realize this and to gain some strength in your own life so you can be the best you, and stop wishing you were different. Follow your heart, cherish the gifts that make you special, respect yourself and people will respect you. If they still don't then screw them! Surround yourself with good people.

Julia Roberts and I at a Benefit in San Francisco, 2008
I am so lucky to be on the arm of one of the most talented movie stars in history.

# DIVAS

di·va **noun, plural di·vas, di·ve**

**A talented, but arrogant or self-entitled female performer**

We have all heard the term diva and used it when talking about a friend who takes too long to get ready or complains about something not being good enough. But there is a huge difference between a friend being difficult and a *real* Diva! Having worked with countless celebrities over the years, of course, I have run into some major divas. As much as I don't like to talk badly about people, there is no way I can write a book about my experiences and *not* mention these women. Before I jump into this shark filled topic and share my personal experiences with some of the world's biggest and best diva's, lets quickly explore the world they live in a bit more to see why they may have become this way.

Celebrities, while they are normal people with extreme talent, in society they are not treated like the rest of us. Many celebrities have an assistant or assistants who cater to their every whim; hairstylists, make-up artists, wardrobe designer, publicist, personal trainer, chef, drivers, managers, and agents telling them how amazing they are twenty-four hours a day. Mobs of cameras wait outside of their homes and follow their every move. If they sneeze rudely, it's on the cover of magazines the next day. If they trip or stumble at an award show, it's replayed a million times on the news that evening. Whenever they show up to a restaurant they don't need to wait, they get seated immediately and often times don't have to pay for their meal. Companies send them free products in the hopes of them being seen using it. They get paid hundreds of thousands, if not millions, to work for a few weeks on a project because they are told they are "worth it." They have dressing rooms filled with champagne, flowers, and food they never even asked for. It is a life of privilege and its understandable how some celebrities can come to "expect" that lifestyle after a while.

It's almost as if the office you work at provided free coffee in the kitchen every day for five years, then one day you came in and there was no longer coffee. You'd speak up, "where's the coffee?" You work hard and deserve to have free coffee! Well, the same sort of entitlement thing happens with the celebrities, only on a much, much grander scale. I'm not saying it's right by any means, but it certainly is understandable after seeing it all first hand.

You never know which celebrity will be rude, mean, demanding and what other ones will treat you like family. I have met some middle grade celebrities that have treated me like a doormat, and yet some of the most famous people in the entire world have been the kindest of all. Some people just let the lifestyle get to them, while others respect and appreciate what they have been blessed with.

The one exception to this rule is reality stars and new music artists. Many of them think they need to have a huge entourage and treat people rudely so they will get respect. They also think people will believe they are more special and it will help them become a bigger star. This is NOT true. From my experience, the biggest stars are often the sweetest people. Maybe because they are secure, know they are talented, and don't need to be demanding. This industry is also run on relationships, so if someone is rude and demanding, no one is going to want to book them on the next gig. Most times, these newbies look foolish and people just don't want to deal with their drama again.

With all of that said, these are who I believe to be the Top Five biggest Diva's I have met. I just hope that by writing this chapter a black car doesn't show up at my door and cause me to disappear forever! Even though I may think they are Divas, it doesn't mean I don't still love them.

### Diva 1) Sharon Stone

It was in New York at the *VH1 Vogue Fashion Awards* 1999 when I first escorted Sharon Stone. This sultry actress, best known from box office films *Sliver* and *Basic Instinct,* was assigned to be on my arm for the evening. I was so thrilled to have the opportunity to escort her that I even did a special shopping trip for a pair of pants I hoped she would think was fun (as mentioned earlier). Buying this pair of silver pants was my big purchase and even though it was on sale, it still was above and beyond what I wanted to spend. I also knew I could only wear them once since they did stand out like a beacon of light. The shirt I wore was one I had worn to my very first show: black short sleeve with the silver buttons. I was dressed and ready for an evening of glamour and excitement.

The second Sharon walked into the venue I noticed nothing but her beauty. I eagerly introduced myself to the two people with her (her make-up artist and a VH1 rep) and then to her directly. Her immediate response to me was very cold. She sternly looked at my face, refusing to shake my hand, and then told me to walk three steps ahead of her at all times and never to look back at her. I was speechless. At first I thought it was a joke, but it was not. I never had anyone speak to me so bluntly and rudely before.

*How the hell am I supposed to keep walking and guide her if I can't look back and see if she is there or not? Does she realize I am there to help her? Should I have introduced myself to her first and then her people? What did I do wrong to deserve such a comment?* These were all the questions I asked myself, as I stood there dumbfounded. It was my first year escorting so I was not sure how to handle the situation. Regardless, I did my best to please her by keeping my head down and do my job. I felt like a bit of a tool with my silver pants rubbing together and my head down as I led the way through the venue. There were many moments where I felt I should just leave and let her figure everything out, but I wanted to be professional. Besides, if I became upset and emotional, I could have been told I was over reacting and not asked back again for another show.

About ten minutes after those candid instructions, her make-up artist pulled me aside and apologized for Sharon's behavior. We chatted a bit and he tried to make me feel better knowing her nasty comment really got to me. His name was Kevyn Aucoin, which meant nothing to me at the time. It was only days later I found out he was the best-paid make-up artist in history and the most talented.

Toward the end of the evening, after Sharon had gotten into her car and left, Kevyn once again apologized for her behavior and invited me to some after party that he and the talent rep were going to. He said the limo was parked out front and ready if I wanted to join them. It sounded like an awesome party and arriving by limo would be a real treat. But for some unknown reason I declined. Maybe it was because I just wanted to hang out with some friends and bitch about how I was treated by Sharon.

From time to time, I saw Kevyn at shows doing make-up for celebrities, such as Janet Jackson, and he always took the time to say hello to me. In May of 2002, I was very sad to find that Kevyn died from liver and kidney failure due to medications he was taking for a lifelong pituitary tumor. It's funny how knowing a person so briefly can affect you so greatly. Even though we only shared some brief moments, I still think of him from time to time and how he took the time to cheer me up.

Eight years later, in 2007, I was asked to escort this Diva again, but this time to the *Independent Spirit Awards*. This event was always a fun show to work and was different because it was held in an enormous tent by the beach in Santa Monica.

I told my supervisor I didn't want to escort Sharon, but she said I was the best person for the job. I have always felt that she is the best escort manager in the country and she always gave me great talent on dozens of shows, so I was grateful. She also handled every show with grace and treated all escorts with respect, which doesn't always happen. She would even go out of her way to make sure none of the escorts would have to arrive too early on show. On many shows, the escort managers are either inexperienced or don't value the escort's time; because we sit for up to six hours doing nothing before the talent even arrives. This serves no purpose for anyone and causes the experienced escorts to not want to work those shows again. So if she really needed me to do something, I could suck it up this one time and not cause a problem. I willing entered 'the trap'.

As I waited for her car to arrive, I told myself the minute she would give me a problem, I would be forced to tell her off. The black sedan pulled up and the transportation organizer announced Sharon Stone had arrived. The car stayed parked for a few seconds. I eagerly waited for what seemed an hour. Amazingly, the minute she got out of the car, she came over to me and gave me a big hug. I thought she wouldn't have recognized me after all these years, but somehow she did. Or maybe this was the "New Sharon Stone." I knew she had gone through some health issues in the recent past, maybe that caused her to change her tune? Maybe she was always nice and the first time I worked with her was just a bad day? I will probably never know the answer and she may not even remember the first day she met me, but I will never forget that harsh tone and glare as she spoke those words. The rest of the afternoon went well and I never mentioned my first experience escorting her.

Personally, I don't care if you are the most famous person in the world or bum on a street corner, no one should treat another human being the way she did. I had done nothing to her and in fact, my job was to be there to help her. All these years later and I am still thinking about it! UGH. This is why she stands out as one of the biggest Divas!

**Diva 2) Diana Ross**

It was such an appropriate title for the show *VH1 Divas: A Tribute to Diana Ross*. I was there to escort the Disco Diva, Donna Summer (as I previously mentioned in the book). This section however is dedicated to Ms. Ross herself! Yes, it was a tribute to a true legend whose voice has entertained us for decades. Being an African American woman in the 1960's and becoming a success, is a huge accomplishment in itself. In addition, Diana Ross had been nominated and won many awards over the past few decades for her talent in acting and singing. In fact, in 2012, she won a *Grammy Lifetime Achievement* award. But from my experience being at this one show, I would certainly classify Diana Ross as a true Diva.

I had been told the only way she would do a *VH1 Divas* show is if it was a tribute to her; so from the beginning there seemed to be a sense of entitlement. I know Donna Summer was not happy with her and threatened to leave and not return the day before the show. It seemed Diana Ross had her own agenda, regardless of what anyone else wanted or what had been scheduled.

When the escorts arrived for our first meeting, a few days before the show, we were specifically told, by two different crewmembers, that when working with Diana Ross we were to *not* look her in the eyes and that no one was to call her anything but Ms. Ross. If someone called her Diana or Diana Ross they would be forced to leave. It had to be Ms. Ross because she would become very upset otherwise. Many of us mumbled throughout the day, "Yes, Ms. DIVA Ross!"

Years later, Diana Ross actually addressed this "misconception" on an episode of *Oprah* saying it was not "required," but it is a respect thing for her. I don't believe this because of the way it was instructed to us, and the fact it had to be mentioned ahead of time in the first place is just ridiculous.

The show was recorded Live to Tape so once it began, we thought it would just be smooth sailing and in two hours we would all be on our way home. This was not the case. Throughout the show, songs were changed, because Diana seemed to change her mind on what she wanted to sing and crew and producers tried to keep up with the adjustments she made. In addition, she decided to sing additional songs not included in the rundown and went completely off script. This made many of the crewmembers unhappy because the show actually lasted HOURS past when it was supposed to end. When it got really late, I heard a few of the union members say that at least they were getting double time and probably going to make a fortune because of her.

One would think it would be a treat for the fans to see this lengthy concert, or at least it should have been. Instead, she would start a song and then in the middle stop and decide to sing something else. By the end of the evening, over half the audience had left, many of which were tired and frustrated. The production assistants ran back and forth constantly moving audience members around to make the theater seem full for the cameras. I think most people walked out wondering what hell had just happened. It didn't seem to faze Diana, but finally after six hours of recording the show, it was over.

## Diva 3) Courtney Love

For those of you who may not know her, ex-stripper Courtney Love's onset to fame was in the Indie Rock scene as a singer for her band, Hole. In addition, she had been an actress in several films even getting nominated for a Golden Globe! However, what really made Courtney's name famous world-wide was her abuse of drugs, on stage anger outbursts, and the terrible loss of her famous rock star husband, Kurt Cobain; who in 1994 was found dead after a self-inflected gunshot wound. *Rolling Stone Magazine* once called her "the most controversial woman in the history of rock."

When I escorted Courtney Love at the *World Music Awards* in 2004, I was well aware of her colorful past. I accepted the notion she might be a difficult diva, but I was up for the challenge since I really didn't want to be close to Whitney Houston that evening (full story to come in the Whitney section). I was well experienced at this point in time and many people around town were realizing I was excellent at handling just about any situation. I had already been notified that my supervisors had received several compliments from celebrities mentioning I was the best celebrity escort around. I felt free to be more of myself instead of the super cautious and insecure man I once was.

I waited by the back entrance with a fellow production crewmember for Courtney to arrive. Usually I waited by myself, but for some reason assigned someone else to wait along with me. It was getting close to the start time of the show and I believe all of the other presenters had arrived. Wondering why I was still waiting, and if she was even coming, I was told her tardy arrival was not her fault. Production had asked her to be a presenter on the show at the very last minute because another celebrity canceled. Knowing this in advanced was great because it instantly shifted my mood from impatient to understanding.

As soon as Courtney entered the building, she seemed unhappy already. I did a very quick introduction as I was pressured to bring her back to her dressing room. The production lady yanked repeatedly on my arm while shouting at me to hurry, always a classy and professional way to handle things in front of a celebrity. I was unaware of what room they were going to assign to her so I just headed towards the dressing room area. Acting cool and together, I quietly asked over the radio what had been decided. Luckily, production had just made the decision and gave me the room number as I reached the backstage area. Someone apparently gave her the very last dressing room there was.

I quickly found this unlabeled room and immediately opened the door for her. Usually on the dressing room doors the celebrity's names are printed in large black lettering on a sheet of paper. It is nothing fancy, but it at least indicates ownership of the room for the evening. She had nothing on her door. The room was super small and looked as if it were a broom closet. It was practically empty with just two chairs and a mirror. I was in complete shock. Courtney was not happy. Her faced hardened. As I waited for her to explode, I double-checked the room number. This was, in fact, the room I was instructed to bring her to. She loudly burst out in laughter, as if this was a practical joke, sternly telling me this could not be her room and it was disrespectful. Well, that is not exactly what she said. It had the same meaning, but with a few 'f' bombs thrown in.

Still a little rattled and confused on why this room was given to her, I told her I would find out what happened and come back with better news. I wanted to be the hero and return with some plush accommodations. I agreed with her that it did seem disrespectful, but I also understood she was a last minute fill in. I wondered, *Why would they even give her a dressing room?* Usually presenters on award shows don't get them because they are reserved just for performers. Presenters can relax and enjoy the green room if they need a space.

Sweat beaded across my forehead as I raced over to the production office, the first of many trips that would soon follow. I confidently barged in, as if someone needed medical attention, causing the three people closest to the door to all look up simultaneously startled. Everyone had been diligently working and scrambling around to do last minute changes for the show that was already in act one. Trying to brush me off for more important tasks, they quickly explained there was nothing else available. I insisted her dressing room looked like a janitor's closet at a shady motel and at the very least someone needed to spruce it up. They continued to work diligently tuning me out.

I rushed back to speak with Courtney afraid for every second that I was gone, it would give her more time to become frustrated with me. Courtney was still on my side though, as I explained the show had begun and everyone was busy making it successful. I followed up with the statement they were sorry about the poor accommodations, but that was the last room available. They wanted to give her something rather than nothing. I thought that seemed a little better than, "They just don't have time to deal with this." Courtney appreciated my help, but still was not satisfied with their response. She told me to tell them she would leave immediately if she wasn't given a real dressing room, as they agreed to in their deal. I ran back to the production office and explained the situation, once again, and how it had made a turn for the worst. This certainly got their attention and they asked me to keep her calm as they were sending someone over in a few minutes.

Courtney and I chit chatted as we waited patiently. Soon enough someone with higher authority did come by and explained the situation to her while doing some major ass kissing. This seemed to do the trick because the dressing room situation was never brought up again. As he was leaving, a writer and producer stopped in to go over the script. There was a lot of disagreeing about changes made to her script and an argument broke out. Courtney became so frustrated she didn't want to talk to any producers, stage managers, or staff. She told everyone to get out, but asked for me to stay. She made it very clear in front of everyone that all of their communication was to be handled through me only! I felt honored, but also very strange because I worried the producers would be mad at me for somehow aligning forces with her. I thought they would wonder why some celebrity escort gets to stay while they were forced out.

Instead, the opposite actually happened. Production staff was very happy because they could focus on the show and I could handle her requests and keep her satisfied. Soon enough everything did simmer down and she seemed very happy; especially after I was able to get someone to bring her a six-pack of Diet Coke. In case you are wondering, no she didn't drink the entire thing, just one can. The rest of the show was peaceful and she was very relaxed and nice to me. Somehow I felt as if she considered me as a friend and there was something about her I really liked and admired.

During this entire evening, I was giving updates to my cousin Jimmy who was at the show. He was visiting from New Jersey and I wanted to give him a glimpse into Hollywood. He loved every second of the evening and was excited to have gone backstage and see celebrities up close. Still pumped with adrenaline, he asked if we could go to the after party. I was very glad he was not exhausted and up for some real fun so we went.

While scouting out the scene on the first floor of the party, Jimmy heard my name being called from the floor above, which overlooked the area where we were enjoying cocktails. Jimmy pointed up with a grin on his face that went from ear to ear. I gazed upward and noticed a woman starring down at me from the VIP section of the party. At first I was not sure who it was, but then my eyes refocused and I realized it was Courtney Love! She waved hello and blew me a kiss. I waved back surprised she went out of her way to scream my name and get my attention. Jimmy nudged me as if I was a huge stud. Then the unexpected happen, as if it were a movie. Courtney actually threw a single red rose down from the second floor. Shocked, I instinctively reached out and caught it with my right hand. I waved back and smiled. She coyly went back to talking with her friends. I have never spoken or seen her again. I didn't take this gesture as a romantic sex thing, but more of a thank you for taking care of me. Looking back though, maybe it was?

This was the perfect end to an evening because everyone was happy. I felt validated for my hard work. I diffused a problem and in the end both sides felt satisfied. Courtney was definitely acting like a diva. However, I guess it's all a matter of what side of the fence you are on. To this day, I am not sure what the allure was, but from time to time I do think of her and wish I had stayed in contact. I am just glad I was on her good side and if I ever need an advocate, I hope she would come to protect me!

### Diva 4) Chaka Khan

I knew nothing about Chaka Khan before she pushed me against the wall in a backstage hallway in Las Vegas. I was not her escort that evening and never had even spoken one word to her when I noticed her barreling down the hallway at the *VH1 Divas Duets* show in 2003. I was speaking with another celebrity escort off to the left side of the hallway when the incident occurred. She obviously was in a hurry to get somewhere. Maybe she didn't see me or maybe she was just a rude bitch, but I felt someone's hand on my back and a huge push which caused me to hit my right shoulder against the wall and for my shirt to rip on its grainy texture. The push was not brutal causing me injury, but more of a "get out of my way" shove, and the rip was just a one-inch tear. I was wearing this new black stretchy shirt, which looking back I probably should not have even purchased. Talk about fashion mistake! Shocked and against the wall, I stood there for a few seconds, but I never heard an apology or even noticed her stop to see if I was alright. I was more dumbfounded and surprised than anything.

Anytime something unique happens to me I always call my best friend James to talk about it. Telling him about what had happened was easy because he happened to be escorting the show as well. I quickly radioed to find his location and we met up so I could tell him face to face. He shook his head in agreement with how crazy it was, we both laughed about it and went our own ways to continue working.

About an hour later James called me on the radio and we met up again because he said he had something important to tell me. As soon as I saw James, he burst into laughter. I asked him what was going on because I hadn't seen him laugh this hard since when we were in high school and did late night pranks around the neighborhood. While gasping for breath in between his laughter spurts, he apologized to me about not believing my Chaka Khan story. I was very confused, but started giggling myself because it was infectious. He said he thought I was being dramatic about the push. He figured she just nudged me and I was exaggerating. Still confused I asked what was so funny. He replied that Chaka Khan just knocked into him so hard he literally fell onto the floor. Again, she didn't apologize or say anything. He was so stunned that it happened after not believing me and happened in the same night. We both laughed hysterically because it was so ridiculous. A violent Diva? Who knew? I am hoping it was an accident and not a large ego pushing, but an, "I'm sorry" would have gone along way. Years later, James and I both still find it amusing this happened and for some odd reason that shirt still hangs in the back of my closet.

### Diva 5) Whitney Houston

Whitney Houston is by far my favorite singer and has influenced me more than any other music artist in history. Even after her tragic death on February 11, 2012, the sound of her voice still touches my soul each time I hear a single note. Many years before I started to celebrity escort, her music motivated and moved me in so many ways. I feel a bit selfish now because there is not a week goes by when I wish she had been given many more years on Earth to create her inspiring music. I am sure everyone agrees that she died way too soon as a singer, actress, mother, friend, and human being. We all lost a true legend.

I will never forget time I was able to watch Whitney perform live during rehearsals and in front of an audience in New York City. It was one of the greatest moments in my life and one I'll cherish forever. The hair truly stood on the back my neck. It felt as if her voice was healing all the wrong in my life and giving me the strength to overcome any future obstacles. Her grace and beauty backstage were gifts for all, as everyone enjoyed her presence and the opportunity to work with her. Standing a few feet from her felt like a gift from God, as both her internal and external beauty radiated.

Even today, I believe this Whitney was the real Whitney Houston, but the Whitney I am about to write about in this section I refer to as the "Crack-is-Wack" Whitney. Unfortunately, everyone knows this Whitney from her notorious interviews where she looked like a frustrated skeletal shell of a person. It was during this time I partly escorted this "new" Whitney. I say I only partly escorted her because partially through the event, I requested another celebrity. I couldn't bear to tarnish the real Whitney memories I had of her. I was not happy about this "Crack-is-Wack" Whitney and felt sadness and anger. This is the only time in my history of celebrity escorting that I dropped a star.

It was the 2004 *World Music Awards*. She was running really late. Her own security seemed frustrated and one guard complained they would never know when Whitney was coming or going. He was always told to hurry up and wait. When she did arrive, there was a lot of chaos and she had on a hood that seemed to hide her from press, or maybe just people in general. She had missed the red carpet and the show was going to begin shortly. I briefly was able to introduce myself, but she just glared at me and said nothing while her team rushed her in the dressing room keeping everyone, including me, locked out. She definitely seemed troubled and not the person I had seen backstage years prior. It was as if her internal light was turned off.

Two guards were assigned on either side of the door as if to protect her from a terrorist. Stunned, disappointed, and locked out from doing my own job, I decided I didn't want to "deal" with all of this drama. It was hurtful to see Whitney behaving this way. I couldn't be exposed to any more idol crushing images. I quickly asked to be reassigned and escorted Courtney Love, a last minute addition to the show, which I discussed previously.

From what I had seen a few times, "Crack-is-Wack" Whitney had a habit of showing up late, or not at all, to various award shows. Producers and crew would scramble around trying to figure out where she was and if she would be coming at all. This was very disappointing for everyone and, for whatever reason she was late or a no show, we were all losing out.

There were a few shows where production would find out at the last minute Whitney was not coming, or she would arrive only several minutes before having to go on stage, giving producer's heart palpations. What surprised me is how productions always catered to her, regardless of the drama. If I was in charge of MTV or a producer of these shows and a celebrity was consistently late, I would stop booking them and playing their music on my channel, until they got their act together. This was the time when MTV was the only major music television outlet and music downloads just started to occur online. It was also before YouTube and other popular sites so if your music didn't play on MTV, your sales suffered. MTV and the producers of these shows seemed to take the high road and give all artists numerous chances.

Regardless of her diva behavior during these years, I was happy to have met the authentic Whitney Houston once during her life and career. Thank you Whitney for all the beauty you have given us and how you have touched millions of people forever. The first day I heard a Whitney Houston song I fell in love with her.

Whitney, I will always love you!

# THE DREADED C WORD

Although gossip is often times fun and interesting to read and hear about, I do like to know the good and positive things celebrities do as well. I love hearing how an actor goes into a burning building to save a family dog or after a disaster how someone flies in to help clean up an oil spill on the beach.

These are all wonderful stories. I have a personal story to share, but it's less dramatic and would not have appeared on your local news. In this story, she did not save anyone's life or raise millions of dollars, but she did change my life simply because she cared. There was no underhanded reason for her kindness, no cameras catching the moment and certainly no one would ever hear about it (so she thought). What I think makes this even more interesting is that she has been dubbed in the press as "The Queen of Mean", a "bitch" and a "terrible boss". What I experienced was more than someone being nice; it was one kind soul reaching out and touching mine.

I was in the midst of my escorting career with dozens of shows under my belt and making my glamorous dreams come true when the realities of life gave me a hard blow. I was a very healthy (so I thought) young man living in New York City, when I began feeling pain in the area around my waistband. It was on the left side only and the ache felt strange. As if a vein, or some sort of tube, was clogged from a small dot of something stuck there and was pushing to get out. Sounds crazy, I know. I do have to admit the movie *Alien* did come to mind at the time this was happening.

I went to my regular family doctor and after examining me, he thought a kidney stone was causing this pain. He told me to drink numerous glasses of cranberry juice and to pee through a coffee filter every day for a week. After about two days, nothing significant happened except the bathroom wall kept getting splatters of urine as droplets bounced off the flimsy filter. It was frustrating because I didn't see any evidence of kidney stones and the pain quickly became worse, almost unbearable.

On the third day of this kidney stone mining expedition, I went back into the office in search for a better answer. My doctor had the day off and another doctor was there to examine me. Within ten minutes he told me I did not have kidney stones, but he instead suspected something else. I was sent to get a CAT scan, which later confirmed his diagnosis. I had TESTICULAR CANCER!

Surprisingly, I handled the news very well and with great strength. I was given a plan by a surgeon and Oncologist, which included three cycles of chemo after surgically removing my left testicle. As soon as I found out I would lose a part of me, questions and fear flooded my head. Everything from, *would I look normal?* To *would I be able to have sex again?* And, *would I be less masculine?* These thoughts began to shred my self-confidence and make me feel less of a man. Depression could have swooped in, but instead I decided I needed to get clear, quick answers and put my pride aside for the time being. Thankfully, I didn't stew in these thoughts for long and I got all the answers I needed immediately.

Everything was set and there really weren't any decisions to be made. I had to start with the treatments and not look back. I was less frightened and more annoyed that a young person, such as myself, had to go through this. At the time I believed cancer was for older people or at least people who had medical conditions before. I was in my twenties and supposed to be invincible from such illnesses. Maybe I was in shock, but for me, it felt as if I had a real bad meeting I didn't want to go to. I wanted this entire thing over with, quickly.

My family was more upset then I was. I could hear the fear in my parent's voices no matter how much they tried to hide it. We had been through a cancer battle before because my mother had very aggressive breast cancer about ten years prior. Thankfully she won. I really didn't remember much except spending a great deal of time with her on the couch and her wig that constantly itched her head. I think these memories are sparse in part because I blocked them out and also because my parents kept my brothers and me away from the hospital with limited information. They wanted to protect us. Now the roles were reversed.

The surgery lasted only about two hours. Everything went as planned. I was told I needed to keep it easy, but to get up and walk around throughout the day. The cut was not in the scrotum as many people think, but it took place in the area between the genitals and belly button on the left side. It was a small incision and would later be hidden by my pubic hair.

I had some good pain medication, which I took exactly as directed to prevent feeling something awful. I really wanted to lie around until fully recovered, but moving around was for the best and so

I did. Some of this was my own fear of doing too much and ripping the stitches open. I still felt minimal pain, but I pushed forward, and within a few days I was walking normally again.

I was lucky to have excellent doctors who reassured me once I healed my sexual desires and abilities would remain the same. They were correct. In fact, let me be so blunt to say the first time I did ejaculate after the operation, it felt as if it were my very first time all over again. It was such an incredible strange feeling, and memories of me with an old sock flooded back. For a few brief seconds, I was a sort of born again virgin! I was relieved everything was functioning like normal, something every man loses sleep over when first diagnosed.

This heavenly moment was short lived though, because two days later I began chemo. For those who don't know, chemo is basically a poison that kills many of the good and bad cells in the body. I would have five days on it, then a few days off, another day of chemo, and then a few days off, then another day and then a few more days off. That was one cycle, and then it would start all over again for two more full cycles.

Just before the first day of chemo, I cut my spiky hair very short so that the hair loss would not seem so dramatic. It didn't really work though because after the third week of chemo, it quickly all came out; including most of my eyebrow hair. It never even occurred to me that I would lose that as well!

I spent much of my time recovering on the couch watching endless amounts of daytime television while popping the numerous amounts of pills I had to take to remain 'normal'. The pills were in those Sunday through Saturday cheap plastic cases senior citizens carry around. Most of the tablets were to prevent nausea and to stimulate my body to want to eat enough food in order to keep my strength up. I was fortunate because the pills worked. My body handled the chemo really well. The side effects were less harsh then the stories I have heard from other people. However, mentally and emotionally, I started to break down. I was in desperate need for something to take my mind off my illness.

Initially I had many goals of what to do with all this "free time," such as writing a book like this one, but between the chemo and the drugs, I felt very strange and could not focus on anything except mindless television. Looking back, I really wish they had Netflix or YouTube because even with forty different channels, I was bored. Toward the end of my treatment, I started to feel stir-crazy from being cooped up in my apartment for so long.

Against the advice from my parents and doctors, I tried to walk around outside for short spurts just to change the scenery and breathe fresh air. They were afraid of me catching someone's germs. I had a very weak immune system and was not supposed to be around lots of people. I was physically beaten down and couldn't go far, but these quick escapes from my apartment prison helped initially. After three months of this and being poked by dozens of needles, I became extremely frustrated and needed more than just twenty minutes away from my apartment.

## *Daytime Emmys* 2001 - New York City

It was toward the end of my treatments when I got a call asking if I was interested in escorting Rosie O'Donnell at the *Daytime Emmys*. I guess the word on the street didn't spread about my condition, so instead of telling a sad story of my unexpected illness, I accepted the assignment hoping I could actually do it. I had spent nearly three months enjoying her daytime talk show. Although some rumors spread she was a bitch in person and difficult to deal with, I wanted to work with her because she was so damn funny. The *Daytime Emmys* had also been my favorite show to work on and I did not want to miss even one year of it, including the opportunity to see my favorite people--the *All My Children* cast. At this point in time, I had watched *All My Children* for over fifteen years. The show was a great escape for dealing with many issues in life; the biggest being my mother's cancer and having grown closer to her by talking about different story lines. In person, all of the actors had always been sweet, and appreciated they were at an award show.

The day finally arrived. Although I felt as if I had been hit by a truck speeding and carrying heavy materials, I was not going to let chemo stop me from attending. I counted the minutes away for this day to arrive. This was my chance to be normal again and to take care of someone else for a change. My parents worried it was too much for me to handle, but I had to do it. I tend be very stubborn sometimes and when my mind is made up on something, I persevere one way or another. I put on my tux and covered my head with a black bandana, making sure to cover every centimeter of scalp previously been occupied with hair. I added some bronzer make-up to my colorless face to make me look human again and headed out to the subway.

As soon as I reached the subway station, a nauseous feeling raced through my body. I put my three-month-old metro card (still with a balance of $9) through the turnstile and walked onto the platform to wait for the next train. My stomach churned, my muscles felt weak. Sweat poured off me. This was not good. How was I supposed to make it through an entire evening if I couldn't even do a simple walk to the subway?

The pain grew worse. I knew what was about to happen next since I experienced it so often during those few months. I immediately stumbled to a trashcan and threw up. It was not the meaty gross kind, but more of a liquid version that made it easier for me to recover. Luckily, I did bring some paper towels to wipe my mouth and a pack of mints I hoped would last me the entire evening. I was embarrassed, but it seemed as if no one noticed or cared. Maybe they thought I was just some drunken guy wearing a tuxedo in the middle of the afternoon. I knew at the very least this would keep people away from me, people who may have germs. Nothing ever seems to faze people at a New York City subway station, though.

I felt a little better and boarded the next train. I only had about a ten-minute subway ride to reach the venue, but I had to get off at two other stops to bless those trashcans with my stomach fluids as well. Luckily everything was timed right and there were no accidents on the train.

In about thirty minutes, I made it to Radio City Music Hall actually feeling better. I immediately headed to the downstairs restroom to check myself over and to make sure I didn't come across as looking sick. I was a little pale since much of the makeup had worn thin, but I felt I looked decent and could come across as healthy. I straightened up, stood tall. I was going to fake it the entire evening no matter how bad I might feel later. No one wants a sick-looking celebrity escort and this was my much-deserved only night out.

**Radio City Music Hall at a Celine Dion special that I worked on. Most of my favorite shows have taken place in this venue.**

About an hour later Rosie O'Donnell arrived. She asked to go straight to her seat. We were still about twenty-five minutes until show time, but she didn't want to bother with heading backstage or running around to the green room. I, of course, granted her request and showed her the way into the house. The minute we entered those doors fans from every part of the room got up from their seats and rushed over to swarm us. I have never seen a crowd this anxious to meet someone. Well, this is not entirely true. Yes, N'Sync, 98 Degrees, and Backstreet Boys all had crowds of eager girls swarm them. I should say instead, I had never seen ADULTS ranging in age from twenty to ninety years, acting like teenagers in such frenzy. People from all ages were climbing over each other to try and get autographs and take pictures. I struggled to move us along as quickly as possible through the sea of people, but there just were so many eager and vocal fans. My arms could only hold so many people back and pushing people away is never an option.

In 1999, I had the pleasure of escorting the three biggest boy bands in one week. In this photo, I'm with 98 Degrees in their dressing room minutes before they were to perform. All my female friends were very jealous!

The odd thing was that people also shouted random connections such as how their grandmother's friend's sister loves her. I thought, *who really cares, that is so far removed what are these fans thinking?* Rosie handled all this chaos with grace and more patience then I expected, or would have myself. This was not something I suspected from someone who is supposedly mean. I only knew her for a few minutes, yet she was nice to me and handled the situation like a pro. She didn't even mumble anything to me like "get me out of here." She simply listened to people and thanked them as we walked.

I quickly realized she got hounded by more fans than bigger named movie stars did. In fact, she had the most fan interaction than any star I had met so far. My theory: People consider many talk show hosts part of their families. They see and welcome these people in their homes every day. These stars seem so accessible. Big movie celebrities tend to be approached less often and less aggressively because there seems to be an unspoken barrier between them and the fans. I think there is something to my theory.

It seemed like it was hundreds of thank you's later, when we reached her seat in the front row, a few feet from the stage. I felt surprisingly good and, for the first time in months, seemed needed and useful. Rosie sat down very happily and the crowd started to back off thanks to the security that finally came in to help. I asked Rosie if she was okay. She turned to me and bluntly asked, "Are you wearing the bandana for fashion or sickness?" I remember that exact question because I was completely taken off guard. I was not used to such forthrightness and, during all this chaos, I actually forgot for a moment I was sick. I quickly responded, "What?"

She asked me the question again. I was honest telling her I was recovering from testicular cancer and hopefully in my finally days of chemo. Instantly, she ignored everyone and everything around her. I could feel her exceptional, focused interest on me. We spoke for at least ten minutes about personal matters and about my feelings and emotions during this difficult time in my life. She also offered me the names of some doctors and any help that she could provide to make sure I got the best treatment possible. She was very sweet, open, and honest. I truly felt she cared about me as a person and was more than willing to help me if I ever needed it in any way. She said she felt honored I wanted to escort her, especially during my recovery.

After that conversation, she never treated me any differently the rest of the evening or mentioned my illness again. She wound up winning for Best Talk Show and Best Talk Show Host, which both were well deserved. There was so much excitement and moving around all night that I did have moments of feeling weak and sick, but they passed quickly. I luckily did not have any more nausea, but I did skip out on the after party because of exhaustion. It was way too much for even me to handle at that point. Although it was always a blast, the comfort of my bed was calling me.

In such a cut-throat industry, it was surprising how generous and kind Rosie O'Donnell was. I don't recall there ever being another celebrity who has showed me that much compassion. The evening was supposed to be all about her since she was nominated for the awards, but she took the time to really share her heart with me.

Rosie O'Donnell has gotten some flack in the past about her quick comments and her candid behavior. She may have said improper things at times. I have seen some of the off the wall moments she has had publicly. However, from my one on one experience, she is a very loving, sensitive, and compassionate person who I am grateful to have met. I can see how stressful her life was and how suffocating that could be every day. Those fans really felt as if she was their best friend and wanted her time. With that much pressure and the constant nagging, I am actually shocked she wasn't a bitch!

Having cancer made me realize anything can happen at any time to anyone, and made me value my relationships with family and friends more. Now, when I see good friends, I hug them. I also make extra efforts to reach out to people I have not spoken to in a while that I think are good people.

**Years after recovering from Cancer, I ran into Rosie at another event and took this picture. I don't think she ever knew how much she meant to me.**

As far as escorting, it made me realize I should be less judgmental and give celebrities some slack. No one ever knows what's happening with others internally. You may see a celebrity and think they have it all, but really they may be in an abusive relationship, lost all their money in the stock market, or have a sick loved one. Moving forward, I tried to give rude celebrities a break and not hold any grudges. I am not saying I want people to take advantage of me, I just would give them extra space and the benefit of the doubt that maybe they didn't realize what they was saying or doing was hurtful. At the end of the day, we all are responsible for what energy we put out into the world, no matter what we are suffering from internally.

After I fully recovered, I went back into high gear escorting at events and made the move to Los Angeles in 2002.

## A Public Service Announcement from Chris Gaida

Having a testicle removed isn't as painful as it sounds. Obviously I know this first hand; I am a proud survivor of Testicular Cancer. Although it did cause some initial minor discomfort, the procedure was far worse psychologically. And hell, the only alternative was to deny it and die.

Men seem to brush off pain and avoid seeing doctors. If I can help even one guy get to a doctor to check that lump down there, then this section of the book is worth it.

Guys who avoid doctors because it is embarrassing or they think it's not a big deal are VERY STUPID! By hearing about my experience with cancer, it's my hope men will listen better to what their bodies are telling them and feel empowered to get help when they suspect something is wrong.

Most men do not like to talk about things that may make them seem weak. I am a man, so I get it, but that way of thinking could kill you. Don't wait! I am no longer ashamed of my battle wound because it is something that truly affects men all over the world, and kills them when it doesn't have too. Men need to express their physical problems to loved ones and see a doctor if they feel pain or discomfort anywhere in their body. If shamelessly admitting I lost a testicle helps anyone, great. No one can argue I didn't have the *balls* to get medical attention immediately, which helped make my recovery quicker, less invasive, and saved my life.

For the women reading this book, I hope you do everything in your powers to convince the men in your life to speak freely about their feelings without judging them. In fact, if you are in a relationship and you notice something wrong or they mention it, I would insist for them to seek medical attention even if that meant withholding sex or nagging them into submission. Trust me that will do the trick!

## Facts

Now that you have read my story there are some important facts about Testicular Cancer you should know:

- No one knows the exact cause of this cancer.

- Men are at a greater risk for getting testicular cancer if they had an undescended testicle anytime in their life.

- Testicular Cancer is the most common cancer in men between fifteen and thirty-five years old! Yes, you do not have to be old to get this cancer. In fact, after age thirty-five, your chances of developing testicular cancer drop dramatically! I was only twenty-six years old when I was diagnosed.

- If caught early enough, you may not need your testicle removed! The longer you wait the worse it can get and spread to lymph nodes and even your brain, such as in Lance Armstrong's case. Once the cancer reaches the brain, it is much harder to treat and requires more invasive treatments.

- Usually Testicular Cancer only affects one side of your body. That means if it is in one testicle it's probably not going to be in the other. The cancer grows up and not usually to the other half of the body.

- Some symptoms can include: Discomfort or pain in the testicle, back or lower abdomen; enlargement of one testicle, swelling or change in feel (with mine I felt a bump, which I thought was a vein); or other symptoms in other parts of the body as the cancer could have spread.

- Testicular Cancer has a very high cure rate and the earlier you get treatment the less invasive treatments can be.

For more information please consult your doctor.

# BACKSTAGE: ALL ACCESS

Very few people have the privilege of getting backstage at *any* event, especially high profile award shows. Reporters have shown some of this world on television, but it's been through a filtered and restricted lens. Celebrities and staff knew the cameras were there. They were on their best behavior. Producers don't just let any reporters or cameras backstage; it is usually only one or two that they trust. Just as with red carpets, you need the proper credential to even take a peek on what happens behind-the-scenes. Luckily for me, as a celebrity escort, I have always had All Access.

During many events, I watched big time producers, directors, actors/actresses, and even top studio executives, get denied admittance backstage. Buff security guards, many former or current police officers, shield these areas with confidence and mostly sheer bulk. Yes, there are some shows where they hire freckle faced wide-eyed young kids my grandmother could tackle, but that's not the norm. Regardless, at every show there are people who try to negotiate or convince security to allow them backstage for one reason or another. Mostly they are fans who may know someone who knows someone, but often they are seasoned professionals. You would think these "big time" people would have a golden ticket, but as a general rule, if they don't have official work backstage, such as present the next award, they are as Suze Orman would say, "So Denied!" It doesn't matter how much they make or how

154

much power they yield, if the producers of the event have not given them access, they need to stay in the house, which most people would think is a privilege itself!

Having a job as a Celebrity Escort is really cool because we get to see and be there for everything. This picture was taken at the *Golden Globes* the day before the show. Everyone was running around setting up the red carpet. It is amazing how many people and how much hard work is required to make everything so glamorous for the cameras.

It is always interesting to see a studio executive, who yields great power, get turned down. One time I saw an executive of a top movie studio trying to get backstage. The security wasn't having it, no matter how powerful the man was or thought he was. Usually I try not to get involved with backstage politics. However, thinking this was a way for me to be nice and get in good with the executive, I told security he was with me. Reluctantly, they allowed him backstage because of my persuasion. I thought I would at least get a thank you, a handshake or something, but this guy just ignored me and went on his way to try to schmooze with some celebrities. About four months later I was escorting at another show and saw him grabbing a drink. I went over to him to say hello and engage in some chitchat. He clearly recognized me and said hello back, but once I started to ask him how he was enjoying the evening, he literally stuck his nose in the air and walked off. It was so dramatic I felt as if I was in a high school play. Two other escort friends noticed this behavior and were shocked by the outright rudeness. I guess he just didn't need me anymore and was too important to even politely excuse himself from my lowly presence. Let's say I am happy he is no longer with the company that gave him power. He was only in that position for a short time. I'm sure there are many other people he did not say thank you to, as well!

## The Backstage Maze

When referring to backstage, it includes dressing rooms, green rooms, holding rooms, quick change rooms, back stage press area, trailers, backstage limo drop off, production offices, teleprompter room, gifting lounge, and walkie room. The backstage area is also the place to find equipment, Stage Managers, band, crew, and the staging area where celebrities wait and are prepped seconds before walking on stage.

Many of these areas are spread out quite a distance. Sometimes, people have to walk a few minutes to reach their destination, travel to different floors or use underground tunnels. This may not seem like big a deal, but there are hundreds of people backstage, large pieces of moving equipment, and the timing is crucial. Most of these shows are live. Ten or even five seconds off is awkwardly noticeable onstage and unforgivable to a viewer watching at home. One of the reasons celebrity escorts are necessary is to navigate celebrities through these mazes and to make sure the talent arrives where they are supposed to be, on time.

The term "Backstage" can be a bit vague, yet most people have some idea of what goes on behind the curtain. The quick shots on news shows and scenes in movies, mostly inaccurately, reflect this coveted area. Let me explain what it is like to be backstage and how everything is laid out. Of course every award show and layout is different, for ease, I will explain the most common set up and what you need to know to "get around".

## Knowing Your Way

Usually, the day before or the morning of an event, there are rehearsals and walk-throughs. Rehearsals are vital to making sure a show runs smoothly. Not only do camera people need to know where to shoot, lighting crew needs to know what to light and when, staff needs to change set pieces and know where to store them, celebrities need to practice their lines, test the microphones, see where the teleprompter is and when to enter and exit. Everything needs to happen at once with everyone or something will stand out as being awkward.

As an escort I am required to know where my talent is exiting and entering, and which routes are best to bring them to and from their seats, dressing room, green room or various other destinations they to visit. Often, what I plan during rehearsal changes by show time because equipment may block a hallway during a set change, or security suddenly decides to lock a door or hallway they didn't during rehearsal. One little thing *not* communicated to everyone on staff can make the difference between a celebrity getting on stage on time or not. This is why, before an event, I always spend a great deal of time walking every hallway and checking every door to where it leads so nothing can take me by surprise. I re-walk all of the possible routes up to ten times before the start of red carpet so I can be prepared and have alternative routes, in case something has changed. I take my job very seriously. Sadly, I know there are plenty of escorts who only find one way to walk their talent and when there is any sort of unexpected situation, they fumble. This is the difference between an average escort and a great escort.

To give you an example about how knowing the location can help out, here is a short story about an event I did at Radio City Music Hall in New York City. Having never worked at Radio City before, I was thrilled to be working there, the home to the Rockettes! When I was a child my mother and Great Aunt brought me to Radio City Music Hall for the first time during the busy Christmas season. The magic of seeing the huge open grand place as a child was one of my favorite memories. Getting to actually see the behind-the-scenes workings of the place, the tunnels and nooks and crannies that only a select few ever get to see was exhilarating.

The venue of course was very glitzy and beautiful. Everything has been polished and cleaned to perfection. Every detail attended to. The difficult part of the venue is the backstage logistics. While a show performed, it's very difficult to walk from one side of the backstage to the other, because there's no room to do it. Most stages/productions leave a back area open for this; however, Radio City Music Hall doesn't have space during these shows. The architect must have been aware of that when designing it because there are three alternative options.

The first option is to take an elevator up to the seventh floor, then climb two flights of stairs, cross over a long hallway, and then go back down to the opposite side of the stage. This involves stairs and an elevator, which makes celebrities in heels very unhappy.

Option two is to go from backstage, along the side of the house, cross through the back of the audience area, come down the other side of the house and head backstage. This, of course, interrupts people enjoying the show because they will see their favorite star walk by. The general public will also mix with the star in the back sometimes, slowing us down while they say hello or try to get a photo. It's not very private and usually not the preferred method although it is technically simple.

The third option, the one most crew members use, is to walk down a small flight of stairs located on either side of the stage to the basement, follow a very long, dirty, winding tunnel until you reach the other side, and then go back up the stairs on the other side. The tunnel is very industrial looking and not glamorous at all! There are also many other hallways that lead off in various directions where people tend to get lost. When going the correct way you pass the hydraulics for the stage as well as other equipment. It reminds me of the boiler room in the *Nightmare on Elm Street* movies, and when I walk the path by myself, I always think Freddy may jump out and get me. Even with that "danger," it is the quickest way to get to the opposite side of the stage, for sure, and to avoid the general public.

In addition to the lack of a sexy atmosphere, it also can be the most confusing route to take as well. During some shows it is not always bright and many times the crew has not added the fancy taped arrows to the ground, pointing people in the direction they should be going. Those arrows have saved me many of times before I was able to memorize the way.

That particular evening, as I was walking through the creepy tunnel, a stage manager desperately came running over to me because he couldn't find his way out. He must have been lost for a while because he was sweating and had a very frantic looked like a lost kid searching for his mother at the mall. The show had already begun and he would get fired if he didn't get up to the stage immediately. Without just one of the stage managers, the entire show could be thrown off. I could hear from the small speaker on his walkie multiple people calling for him as he didn't even have his headset plugged in properly. Their voices actually echoed in the tunnel, *Where are you? What the hell is going on?* He paced, visibly shaking as he pleaded for my help. Within one minute, I was able to lead him back up the correct side of stage he needed to be at. I'll never forget this because I was surprised a well-paid stage manager could not find his way around the venue. I only hoped he would not get lost again, but I am sure he was so stressed out, he didn't come down in the tunnel area again that night.

Later, that same evening, I rescued another lost man. But this time I knew his name very well, Ricky Martin. It was at the height of his initial U.S. fame, when he was living, "Living La Vida Loca." We were told there would be a "special guest" performance, but production didn't tell us who. When award shows don't want a particular celebrities name announced to the public they refer to them as a "special guest." They are often afraid if the crew is told that information then it will be leaked to the press and the surprise will be ruined. Sometimes production uses a top-secret code only the FBI could crack (the celebrities initials), but usually they are labeled on all the paperwork just as a special guest.

Due to his huge fame at the time, I was sure the "special guest" was going to be Ricky. I had been a huge fan of his, not just because of his music, but because I could tell he was a very good person. That statement makes me laugh now because you never know until you really meet someone what they will be like. I first heard him speak in an interview in 1996 on a cassette tape my college roommate brought back from his semester abroad in Argentina. I was so intrigued by his speaking voice, how he phrased sentences and his kindness about life.

Ricky performed a song during the evening and then seemed to vanish immediately after. I knew he still had to be at the venue somewhere because his car had not left and was waiting for him. Being a fan, I decided to make it my mission to meet him. There was a rumor Radio City Music Hall had a hidden dressing room used during various shows in the past, so I decided to start my search there. The problem was, it had been hidden to me as well! I knew the venue very well so I knew at least where to not look.

After about fifteen minutes of searching tunnels and different floors, I had to give up because I needed to get back to my assigned talent still sitting in the audience. Disappointed, I turned a corner to head towards the stairwell and literally bumped right into Ricky Martin. He was very tall and with another Hispanic man who I later found out was his manager. *Boy, was that perfect timing,* I thought. Mesmerized, overwhelmed and shocked, I stuttered the worst phrase you could say to a celebrity, "I am a huge fan." Shy and embarrassed I sunk my head down low.

He said, "Thank you, but we are a little lost in finding our way out." It was not the response I expected, but then it dawned on me he was asking for *my* help. This was actually something I could help them with and I could be of more use than a babbling fan.

I instantly popped my head back up and said, "I'll help you get out of here. It is a maze".

Proud that I was perfect for this job, I escorted them through the hallways and out the back entrance to his waiting car. Along the way there had been some small talk, but I had no idea what to say and I was still star struck. They both thanked me for my help and were off to rule the world with his music. I was grateful I had the opportunity to help him, but the only reason I could was because I had learned the ins and outs of all the hallways earlier. Something so simple became a badge of honor for me. Hell, I was able to tell people I helped Ricky Martin find his way! Sure, I didn't discover a new drug for science or invent something, but my friends were fascinated and it made for one hell of a cocktail story. Especially when at the time, he was the most famous person in the world.

Many years later, in 2010, I was able to meet Ricky and his manager a few more times at shows such as the *Grammys*, and officially escort him to the annual television special *Home for the Holidays*. Both Ricky and his manager greeted me like family and it felt as if I had known them both forever. Ricky gave me some advice about what he learned while writing his book. At the time his book *ME* had just hit stores and he was so awesome in autographing a copy, which I really enjoyed reading.

The great thing about Ricky is that he is a very kind man and never acted like a superstar. In fact, Ricky and his manager are two of the sweetest and most genuine people I have met in and out of show business. They work harder than most, yet they treat people like family and always respect other people's talent and time. For me, Ricky Martin is a real super star, icon, and role model for us all. I hope the next generation of young people discover and enjoy his catchy and gifted body of music, and I look forward to any new music he creates in the future.

**Me and Ricky Martin**

## Dressing Rooms: Not What You Think

Probably the most private areas backstage are the dressing rooms. In fact, they really are the *only* private areas you will find where very few crew have access. Having this VIP area and big named stars you would think the dressing rooms would be this incredible luxurious space where every celebrity gets one and hangs out together while sipping champagne. This is not the case.

1) Only a few celebrities are assigned to dressing rooms at award shows. In order to get one they would need to be presenting or performing and even then, they would only get it if they *need* to do a costume change or their agent fights enough for them. If they are wearing the same dress as they were on the carpet, then most likely they will not get a dressing room. Men usually don't have access to a dressing room unless they are performing. At award shows, there are just not enough to go around and it's also better to have as many celebrities in their seats for audience shots.

2) Dressing rooms are usually just a small space with a couch, mirror, and maybe two chairs. The space usually looks a lot like dressing rooms used for plays or high school productions. They have those white cinderblock walls. Often, they are cramped. Four people can hardly fit into these rooms at once. The production staff usually adds flowers, some nonalcoholic drinks, fruit platter and other prepackaged munchies like potato chips, to make the rooms more comfortable for the stars. These amenities can vary depending on the show. Some shows have more plush spreads while others have rooms with just bottled water and a bowl of M & Ms.

One of the large dressing rooms I have found.
This is plush compared to what most celebrities get.

3) Some dressing rooms have bathrooms, but surprisingly, most do not.

In many cases celebrity restrooms are NOT glamorous and not private.
Everyone uses the same ones like here at the *Independent Spirit Awards.*

4) Occasionally, there is a television with a live feed of the show so the talent can watch from the room. Without a TV to watch the show, they must rely upon their escort or a stage manager to give them updates. The norm is for a stage manager or escort to give them a ten-minute warning and then pull them to walk to the stage. If they have a television in their room, then they will at least have a better idea of when to expect the warning.

5) Regardless of the show or venue, I have never seen a big cut out star on the door of a dressing room; as depicted on TV shows and films. You know, one like Miss Piggy had on her dressing room door on *The Muppet Show*. Usually there is just a white piece of paper with their name on it, if that! This surprised me when I first started escorting.

6) Most celebrities don't seem to really care about their dressing rooms, they're usually just happy to get one. Yet, I have seen others make the most of a drab situation. For example, Elton John's assistant has been known to show up hours before Elton to make his room more comfortable. I'm not sure if it is a request from Elton or something his assistant believes should be done. Regardless, someone from his team has brought in boxes of stuff such as materials, pillows, extra mirrors, and all sorts of fancy extravagances, all so they can be enjoyed for the mere four hours the talent is in there.

7) For many of the larger shows, there are usually trailers parked outside for some of the musical artists. I believe this is mainly a space issue because all the dressing rooms are full. These trailers are much nicer

than the dressing rooms. However, many stars rather have the dressing rooms so they can be closer to stage and the green room. The *American Music Awards* park these vehicles outside on the roof of the parking garage next to the press tent several hundred feet from the stage entrance. Celebrities have to take a short elevator ride, walk across the blocked off street, and into the building to get to the stage. I personally don't think it is a big deal since it's only a three-minute trip. However, it can really suck on the rare occasions it does rain. This happened when I escorted Enrique Iglesias at the *American Music Awards* in 2011. We were stuck in his trailer for most of the show, instead of being able to walk around outside and enjoy the day. He didn't seem to care one bit and his positive attitude and smile put everyone at ease.

8) You sometimes hear the big requests and crazy demands from celebrities. While this might be part of their requirement for giving a concert or doing their own show, in my experience, I have not found this at award shows. There have been some minor requests such as such as Mariah Carey and honey or Courtney Love wanting Diet Coke. But many times I find it's not the celebrity asking for these items. Instead, it is a person on their team requesting it. Many times a celebrity will ask for a particular item like iced tea. When certain crew members hear that, every time that person comes to an event they work, they tell everyone they must have iced tea for them. Mostly people want to stand out and make the celebrities happy. Occasionally, this is an effort to do a good job, but mostly it's to kiss up. It gets frustrating because you don't really know if a celebrity has a specific request or if it's just something they asked for once. Sometimes you also get the assistant or manager desiring

something themselves, but saying it's for the celebrity. These the reasons why there is a great deal of food wasted and unopened drinks at these events. From my experience, it rarely has to do with the celebrity and, in fact, I've heard many times the star question why they always have a certain item or why there are so many of items in their dressing room.

A typical table inside a star's dressing room.
Not too fancy but plenty to drink for one person!

## Dressing Rooms: Off Limits

Usually there is tight security for the dressing room hallway. Certain celebrities have their own security wait outside their dressing room door, as well. On a very rare occasion, security gets breeched. Such as the time I was escorting Jessica Alba to an event. After changing, she came out of her dressing room to talk to me in the hallway. Mid conversation some guy walked by us and into her room. She asked me who that was. I did not have a clue and called security. He was escorted out. It was very strange because he walked right by us and into the room not saying a word to either of us. When I saw him do it I thought it must be someone she knew because he did it without hesitation. Luckily, security took care of it quickly and the man was kicked out of the event. I believe he just wanted an autograph. But how scary would it have been if she were alone in the dressing room with him. This is why tight security and privacy are important.

At awards shows, dressing rooms are rarely ever locked, even when there are diamonds and expensive dresses. Usually someone stays in the room to watch these items and make sure no one walks off with them. If someone does lock the room, it's a gamble because we need to find the proper person with a key. Keys are not given out because then they would tend to go missing. During one show, I was walking down the dressing room hallway and heard this young lady (maybe twenty-two years old), yelling at people. She headed in my direction and I had no idea what was going on. Breathless, angry, and panicked she asked me for a key to the dressing room. I've never had a key at any show. There is usually a person in charge of dressing rooms that carries a spare key just in case someone accidentally gets locked out. A few times, I have been asked for a safe or a way to lock the door. Then I would radio over to the dressing room coordinator to tell them we are locking the door and to stay close in case we need access to the room quickly. Here I was just walking down the hall, yet this young lady yelled at me to open the door for her. Clearly she locked herself out.

Normally I would have helped her and the spiritual side of me said that I *should* help her, but she was so rude. Angry at her exploding at me, I simply said, "I don't have one" and then walked past her. I asked a fellow escort who was standing in the hallway, as if a tornado just went through, what that was all about. She stated the girl was Mariah Carey's Assistant and that she locked herself out of Mariah's dressing room. She apparently needed something for Mariah while she was on stage rehearsing. It was interesting to see how high strung someone was to make a celebrity happy. I understand being in a hurry, but that was crazy behavior. The bad part in all of this is she made Mariah look bad! Regardless if it was Mariah yelling at her assistant or her assistant overreacting, that's how rumors start. Celebrities need to be careful because whoever works for them could unknowingly damage their reputation.

In 2010, I did escort Mariah Carey to the *Independent Spirit Awards* and she was very nice. Her movie *Precious* was being nominated all over town and she was reeling with excitement. This was also the time when rumors started that she was pregnant. My thoughtful action certainly didn't help things. At the end of the evening I actually was the person who arranged for her car to pick her up from a back entrance and escape as the press gathered at the official exit. I didn't want her to be hounded by the pubic or the press and for her to enjoy the rest of her evening stress-free. The back entrance had no one there, so I thought it would make her departure super easy. Rumors swirled she exited out the back because she was pregnant and it was too much walking around for her, but in reality I arranged it.

On a side note, her "dramatic" assistant was not there. I imagine she is now doing something else with her life that I only hope is peaceful.

## Gift Lounge: Just Like Christmas

One of the most talked about backstage areas at award shows are the infamous gift lounges. Back when I started escorting, these lounges were larger and had better, more expensive gifts then they tend to now. I believe in 2006 the government did a crackdown and stepped in after realizing many celebrities were not declaring these items on their taxes. In addition, with the economy tanking, companies to cut back on many luxurious gifts, so lounges suffered. Don't feel bad for the stars because these rooms *still* have many expensive and amazing items, depending on the show. These gift lounges are heavily guarded and, typically, even celebrity escorts are banned from crossing over into these heavenly rooms. Many times, I have gotten in because the celebrity wanted my help carrying their bags while others wanted me with them at all times.

The gift lounge for the *2011 American Music Awards.*
Pretty spacious and ready for stars to get free products.

Usually the gift lounges are in a tent or large room at the venue. Celebrities are encouraged to browse the room of free stuff after they rehearse or after they finish the red carpet, but always before the start of the show. During the show, these rooms are often closed. The escort brings their talent to the door where they check in. We are usually told in advanced if our star is cleared for this room. Not all celebrities are on the list or allowed in the gift lounge! The list is usually restricted to presenters and performers of the show. Rarely, if a big name comes by they will let them in even, if they are not on the list. This always surprises me as I have seen people who I thought were big names and should get in, only to be turned away feeling disrespected. Why is this you may ask? The gift lounge is full of vendors from various companies who rent a space to give out these free items. In turn, not only do these celebrities get to wear, play with, or consume these items, but also pictures are taken of the person with the product. These pictures are then used by the companies to promote their products. Many times they have a limited supply of products to give out. And of course, they want to give those products to the select celebrities they think will help advertise their brand the best.

In these magical lounges there's an array of items ranging from jewelry and sunglasses, to board games, exquisite food, clothing, video games, the latest cell phone that's not even out on the market yet, trips, and even mattresses! These companies also hire assistants to walk around with the celebrities to hold their bags and help them with any questions. Stars can opt out of photos with specific companies and can pick and choose what products they are interested in. Many gift lounges have a charity or two where if they sign something, take a picture or even play one video game, the company will donate X amount of money to a specific charity. Typically I have found it to be $1000 per signature, but it can vary. Once the celebrity has the items they want, they may leave the bag or bags with the assistant and are given a tag. This sort of coat check method is in place so the star doesn't have to carry everything around or be seen in public with bags of free products. At the end of the evening, the celebrity gets into his or her car and the items are placed in the trunk. On some rare occasions the items are shipped to their house, especially if they live in another city.

**Products featured in the lounge at the *2011 American Music Awards***

I have drooled over many of the goodies in these rooms, but my all-time favorite gift I have wanted for myself has been the AMC gift card. Basically, you would bring this card to any AMC theatre and get unlimited free movies for one year! The only time I have ever begged for something was for this card, and no, I didn't get it. Dang it! I am not sure why I want it so badly, I just do! I love AMC theaters and being able to just walk into any movie anytime I want for free would be awesome.

I have been lucky and grateful to receive a few free gifts over the years from gift lounges.

One of the nicest items I have scored was from one of the *TV Land Awards* shows. I was speaking with a security guard at the gift lounge and mentioned how I really liked this leather picnic basket backpack. It had cloth napkins inside, plates, wine glasses, a cutting board, metal utensils; it all fit neatly into a leather backpack. I had worked with him on several shows, but barely knew him. I don't even know his name! He told me to go to the back of the tent, suspicious, but anxious to get a free gift, I ran around the tent. When I arrived in the back, he peaked out and handed me the picnic set I was just talking about. I was so thrilled I wanted to scream with joy. This guy was great. I just mentioned I wanted one, so he made it happen. I am sure he could not have just taken it. I needed to make sure no other escorts saw I got this cool gift, or everyone ask questions. Many vendors have given free gifts to the escorts at a few shows, but that was on rare occasion.

To this day, it is one of my favorite things I own. I bring it on various day trips. One unusual place I take it with me is to the Hollywood Forever Cemetery. The cemetery does this unique thing where they show movies on the weekend outside in the middle of the cemetery. Everyone lies on blankets in the grass while the films are shown on a mausoleum wall. Nothing is more fun than watching a Hitchcock movie by his actual grave in the cemetery at night—especially when you have a nice picnic set up.

## Green Room/Holding Room

As I mentioned in the definition chapter, the holding room and green rooms are two hot spots, which are usually overflowing with celebrity activity. Often, escorts on many shows are, once again, asked to wait outside when these rooms fill. In most cases, escorts can go in if they need something or to speak with their talent, but no lounging around allowed. I understand this and respect it.

The holding rooms are very basic and used right before the celebrity needs to go on. I never bother talent once they are in there because I understand they need to rehearse or gather their thoughts and speak with the stage manager. Once I hand them off to the stage manager I take a back seat and wait. Stage managers are extremely good at their jobs and at handling a great deal of pressure and stress. They need to prep the celebrity and then send them out. As soon as that person is on stage, they are already on to the next celebrity.

The Green Room at the *Emmys*. This is where Ashton Kutcher and Charlie Sheen met for the first time after the whole *Two and a Half Men* incident.

175

The green room is usually the most stylish place of anything backstage. This is further from the stage then the holding room, but still pretty close. When shows don't have holding rooms, the celebrities are brought from the green room to stage. It is there for them to eat, drink, relax, chat, and watch the show together. The green room is where many stars meet each other for the first time. Usually this is a fun encounter where numbers are exchanged and even dates arranged. I was present for one of the most interesting and stressful meetings ever.

The Press Green Room, surprisingly nicer than the Green Room.

## 63$^{rd}$ Annual *Primetime Emmy Awards* 2011 - Los Angeles

I was asked to make sure the newsworthy Charlie Sheen was enjoying the event and to attempt to get him to attend the gift lounge. For months, he had been one of the top news stories because of his erratic behavior and comments. Then in March 2011, he was fired from the hit sitcom Two *and a Half Men* where he played a leading role.

As I stood next to Charlie outside the NOKIA Theatre downtown, he seemed to have "tiger blood" still running through him as he puffed on numerous cigarettes and wandered back and forth while talking with his team. We were in an area shielded from the public, but drew a great deal of attention from some of the crew who watched, hoping something interesting would happen. I stayed close to his side with my mission in mind. Charlie knew I wanted to bring him to the gift lounge. I told him after introducing myself. He agreed to, but was not ready to go at that moment. A member from his team said I could and should stay close by them until he was ready because it could be at any second.

**Emmys Waiting to be Won Backstage**

177

Several cigarettes later, Charlie told me he wanted to go to the green room before heading to the gift lounge, so I led him into the backstage area. I had been in the green room a few minutes prior and surprisingly it was empty. For this show, the green room was actually immediately backstage and it wasn't a room, just a large area sectioned off with black curtains. It had two or three tables with food such as chicken skewers and cookies on it as well as many couches and TV monitors broadcasting the live show. There were two entrances into the green room, one on each side of the corner that faced where we entered. I directed him to the left entrance, as I stood back ready to head to the restroom in the opposite direction. As I waited to make sure that they got into the green room, I noticed Ashton Kutcher out of the corner of my eye. He was walking along the other side of the green room about to head into that door. Neither man could see each other, but I foresaw a possible train wreck. Ashton had taken the lead role on the show Charlie was fired from; the two had not seen each other since this was announced. I darted over to the green room just in time to see Ashton's face when he noticed Charlie sitting on the couch a few steps away from him. Charlie had not yet noticed Ashton behind him. The green room was still empty except for Charlie, Ashton, a few of their team and me. I believe there were seven people total in the room and I had a clear sight- -I was curious on what would happen. Ashton looked very nervous, as I would have been, not knowing how Charlie would handle the situation. I could feel Ashton's tension. This probably lasted about thirty seconds when either someone told Charlie or he realized a person was standing behind him. Charlie turned his head. Upon seeing Ashton and stood up. Waiting for a scene from *Rocky* to occur, I was surprised when Charlie politely said hello and shook his hand. They both awkwardly laughed as I watched from several feet away. I felt like a fly on the wall, but thought it was awesome that I was there for this first time encounter. It was great they both were a good sport about it all because it easily could have gone badly.

At the *Primetime Emmys*

## Even Celebrities Get Star Struck

The biggest surprise I found backstage is that celebrities are huge fans and get star struck too. There are always moments where I hear celebrities congratulate each other and tell each other they are big fans of their work. And most truly are. There are IPhones snapping pictures and introductions made between family members. I always assumed this would not be the case. I guess I thought because celebrities are celebrities they know each other, or wouldn't care to get a picture, but they too are touched by others' work.

A perfect example of this was when I was escorting Susan Sarandon at an event in New York City. She was with her daughter Eva Amurri, who at the time was a young girl. After walking the red carpet Susan asked if I could do her a huge favor. One of her favorite music artists was there and she really wanted to meet him.

"Is there any way you could introduce me to Sting?" I smiled at her question because I knew where his dressing room was and could easily walk her over. Noticing we still had plenty of time before the show began, I told her to follow me. I lead the way and was relieved to find Sting's dressing room door open. Peeking in, he seemed not to be busy. I knocked, then made the introduction. Susan was ecstatic. She even asked to take a few pictures with him. After a couple of minutes, we walked out. Susan wore a huge grin on her face. I knew that grin well. Meeting *her* caused me to have the same one.

Days later, I was walking in Soho, a section of lower Manhattan. Who did I see across the street? Susan Sarandon and her daughter Eva. Without thinking, I foolishly screamed "Susan," and waved excitedly. Susan, without looking and probably thinking I was a crazed fan, ducked into a cab. Eva looked over and noticed it was me, but she was pulled into the cab before she was able to tell her mom.

I laugh now when thinking about that moment because screaming a star's name across the street could cause a mob scene. I was just caught up in the moment I guess. I ran into Eva a few years ago on the red carpet at a Trevor Project fundraising event in Los Angeles, and she said she actually remembered me from all those years and that situation! It's always nice when you're remembered, even if it *is* for yelling across the street.

## Backstage is Not Always Glamorous

The biggest misconception about backstage is that it's glamorous. Many people think it is just like the red carpet and the hallways are lined with beauty. This is not true. In fact, not only are the hallways plain and often bland, but in some cases they're gross! There have been plenty of shows where dirty dishes and trash lay in the corners backstage, or in the kitchen areas celebrities are required to walk through. There are empty boxes also clutter the space. Sometimes, I have to carry a girl's dress train because the floors are filthy. Many times celebrities have to walk over cords and even straddle equipment. This is something no cameras show.

This is not only true in the hallways and backstage, but also in press areas where celebrities talk about winning their precious awards. Below are two pictures I think you would find interesting. One shows what you see on television. I then moved the camera one foot to my left and you can see what people at the event actually see. The set looks great, but it is literally in a parking garage! This one happens to not be very dirty, but it's still shocking to know this the reality of what celebrities have to walk through to get the pretty interview done.

**A Press Area Backstage as Seen on Camera**

**What the Press Area looks like for Celebrities.**
The glamour is stripped away when you see that it is in a parking garage and there is no beauty surrounding everything that is not on camera.

**At the *Daytime Emmys*. There really are no frills backstage.**

People backstage are not always glamorous either! Politics often comes into play, making some people really ugly. Many of the same co-worker and supervisor issues faced in an office or at a place of employment are the same ones I face behind-the-scenes at award shows. There are those people who will not like you no matter what you say or do to try to change that, and there are those who you click with from the start. There are politics, backstabbing, and bad bosses to deal with in all professions.

In the entertainment industry though, it sometimes seems everything is heightened. There's a great deal of pressure in these jobs. People looking for reasons to get rid of you and ask questions later, if at all. The pressure is sometimes overwhelming and your family and friends don't understand the cut-throat nature of it all. The instability of going from one job to another in this freelance driven world is frightening.

It's a constant battle to stay true to yourself and be who you are. Like any job, sometimes when you stick your neck out, it can get cut off. It is rare someone will stand up for you even though they know you are right. People at most jobs want to stay under the radar because they have learned drawing attention to oneself is the quickest way to cause themselves trouble. Fortunately or unfortunately, I have not and will not be that person. I believe when I am hired, I am so for my experiences and education.

Over the years, I worked numerous events and have always gotten along with every stage manager--except for one. Although we never had a problem with each other personally, I have witnessed her throw many escorts under the proverbial bus, blaming them for things that were actually due to poor communication on her part. I have also noticed she tends to blow things out of proportion, escalate problems and exaggerate the truth. To me, she's an adult bully who enjoys emotionally pushing people around. She's not liked at all by most escorts. I have even heard many celebrities complain how fake and bossy she tends to be. Her usual MO is to create drama so that she can "save the day." This is truly annoying because there would be no drama if she were not involved in the first place. It's always shocking when producers continue giving her work. I have to believe they don't really see what she's like in action as they are focused on other things.

Unfortunately, many good escorts have been discarded because of this woman's own insecurities and outright lies. We should be working as a team and have the best interest of the show and celebrities in mind.

Once again, there is always one person who makes things difficult for many. One bad experience I had was with the show's security. It was at the *American Music Awards*. The evening security team continued letting the wrong people past certain check points. People like myself, were not allowed in the house where I needed to be throughout the show. I complained to my supervisor because I did not want to be responsible if something happened later because of my lack of access. My supervisor tried to get in as well, but was denied by security. An argument started between the two of them. This was a serious problem because we were not able to do our jobs effectively. The few times occurred at other shows was because the person in charge of security either gave wrong information or did not explain it well enough. I have no idea what the problem was in this situation. Since this was a live show and we needed to get other things done, we could not focus on this one issue and just tried our best by working around it.

At the end of the evening my talent left. I was asked to find other talent remaining at the venue and make sure they got to the party or to their cars safely. I could have easily gone home at this point because my job had technically been done, but I was helping out to make sure everything was handled to the very end. I searched all the dressing rooms and the talent was either gone or someone else was escorting them out. The last remaining place was the press tent so I went to the roof of the parking garage where it was located to search for any straggling talent.

When I reached the doors, a security man rudely told me I could not enter the press area. I showed my all access badge and explained I still had a job to finish. Thinking it was not a problem and just a misunderstanding, I walked into the tent only to have the security guard dodge in front of me to physically block me. He asked me what I was doing. I once again told him I needed to do my job, but this time more confidently. I was curious about why he had a problem with an area I have had all access to all day. He told me there was no talent in there anymore and I could not go in. I asked why. He simply said Justin Bieber was being interviewed. I told him I understood, but there obviously still is talent in there if Justin was in there. He told me Justin wanted his privacy. So I said I would not go into the room he is being interviewed in, but I needed to check the rest of the place out for other talent. (The press tent was actually a huge space made up of a large room with several smaller closed off rooms inside. When an interview is happening, they are pulled into one of the smaller rooms. There are several different reporters in the press tent, but they all have separate rooms. I wanted access to the main large rooms so I could see if any celebrities, other than Justin, were still around.)

He insisted, in a condescending tone, I could not go in and told me I needed to leave. Something felt wrong. This had never happened to me at any of the one hundred plus events I had worked. I did not want to just turn my back and leave because if there was more talent left and if something should happen, I could be the one blamed. In addition, to being completely honest, I was now pissed someone was speaking to me so rudely and treating me as if I wasn't good enough to speak with him. He was treating this situation like he was a dictator and didn't even need to explain anything to a peon like me.

Knowing there were two entrances, I decided not to argue any further with him and asked for his name so I could tell my supervisor later. While all this was happening, three other escorts showed up trying to do the same thing as me--their job. I walked away frustrated, but headed straight over to the other entrance. There was another security guard standing there. He acknowledged me and I walked right past him with no problems after he noticed my all access credential. I was about three feet in the main room when out of nowhere, I was stopped by the same security guy who had been at the front entrance. He had run from the other entrance to this one to make sure I would not get in. This felt personal now and his behavior was beyond rude. I explained I had zero interest in Justin Bieber and he couldn't block an entire area off just because one celebrity was in one room. He rudely barked at me that I needed to leave and I was not allowed to enter the tent again.

I decided to walk away and not to argue any further because it just wasn't worth it. I really was ready to leave much earlier and was only trying to be responsible by making sure everything was wrapped up. I went to see my supervisor to explain what had happened and I could not be accountable for anyone still left there. She told me to not worry about it so I left. His rudeness and unprofessional behavior was uncalled for. Even if there was some weird exception and reason for an entire area to be blocked off (over six rooms) for one celebrity, that could have been explained to me the first time, very nicely. Instead, he was on a power trip because he was security and he abused it.

The story doesn't end there! About a month later, I was working a show where the same security guard happened to be working. After seeing me there he immediately went to one of the producers of the show and said something bad about me to try to get my fired. I later found out allegedly he made up some story of me trying to sneak in so I could meet Justin--as it was explained to me from another party the next day. Trust me, I had zero interest in that!

I never did get fired. I tried to explain to the producer what the real issue was but she didn't care because she was busy with the current show and nothing was said again. She also did know I was good at my job having had worked numerous shows for her before. I still worked both of those shows the following years so maybe everyone had been aware of his "god" complex. Maybe he was insecure because he didn't know what was happening and there were many complaints about security all night. I later found out he was actually one of the guys in charge of security. WOW, the fact anyone would trust him to be in charge still amazes me.

Just as in an office or at any other job, there is always one person who tries to ruin it for others. There's always politics and oppressive people to work with. It's difficult to try to highlight someone else's bad behavior. Often, it can get turned on you. If you have experienced this first hand, I feel your pain. I wanted to make sure everyone reading this book knows no matter what profession, this type of injustice occurs. The grass is not always greener so stay strong!

## Befriend Your Local Security Guard

Taking the time to say hello to the security personnel is very important for an escort, yet not many do. Escorts are often focused on their talent or overwhelmed with responsibility they don't reach out to meet the people they work with closely. In addition, I have noticed some escorts get a little nervous around security, for whatever reason. I used to when first escorting because I felt incredibly lucky to be at these events and a little unworthy. Security is present for us as well; we are all on the same team and want a safe, fun event. Many times things happen at events where I need to rush a particular celebrity somewhere. Knowing security means I pass checkpoints quicker, both high and low secure areas. When I need to use the quickest possible route, a security guard with me makes everything easier.

For instance, during the 2012 *Golden Globe Awards*, I had the responsibility to escort worldwide mega hit entertainer Madonna to her dressing room and back stage. Madonna has one of the biggest followings on the planet and sneaking her past people is a challenge. At the last minute, one of the talent team members asked me to bring her through the back of the house, which was rather crowded. Minutes earlier, I had scouted the venue and found a route I thought would be the safest and quickest for us to travel. I already had asked security to clear the lobby area and requested extra security to walk with us. All were in place and the lobby was empty; however, one talent team member insisted we travel through the crowd. I tried to explain the more secure route, but she wouldn't listen. So we went through the very crowded house with Madonna two steps behind me. Everything worked out, but it was stressful and a bit of a hassle for her as we squeezed our way through with hundreds of people gawking.

Many times bigger named celebrities hire their own personal security to insure their safety at these events. Usually this is for music artists or an actress who has been receiving threats. Sometimes it's one person. Other times it can be three or four guards. Being friendly with these guys is essential to having a good escorting experience. They need to feel comfortable with you and your abilities. Although an escort's job is not to act as security for the celebrity, it is helpful to communicate with them so they know where you are headed in advance. They should know you can handle a crowd.

At first, these guys often come across as rude or very serious, but once they know you are smart and on their side, they treat you with respect. Sometimes security call you the night before to explain a few details and probably to feel out your personality. The first time this happened, I was to escort Christina Aguilera at a benefit in 2004. Her security personnel immediately introduced himself. He asked questions about me and what the plans were for the following day. It was very intimidating at first. But I quickly realized he wanted to make sure I am a trustworthy. I gave a quick overview of my experience and explained the latest schedule. He immediately became mister friendly. The next day greet me with a handshake and smile.

Remember, it's their necks on the line if even one minor security issue arises. This is why I always give any personal security guard I meet my phone number ahead of time. I want them to know they can reach me during an emergency if one occurs. Also, I do believe it makes them more comfortable knowing they have my information. If something happens they think is my fault and it affects their client, they can reach me days later.

Fergie, Paris Hilton, and Julia Roberts have some of the most talented and nicest security guys in the biz. They are a pleasure to work with. Nasty security guards make it seem as if the celebrities are difficult and then no one wants those particular people around. As I mentioned before, people need to be careful with who they surround themselves with, especially in Hollywood.

## Backstage is Fun

It's not all drama backstage. Most of the time, it's a fun experience with lots of interesting, hardworking people trying to make the producer's and director's visions come to life. I have met many great people, seen some incredible costumes up close, and even hung out with some fun animals, even green pigs! In fact, after a few years of working backstage, I felt as if I was Kermit the Frog with some of these unusual acts!

One unique experience I had was at the 2009 *Independent Spirit Awards*. As I mentioned previously, the show usually takes place by the beach outside in the afternoon in February. Since it's Los Angeles, the weather is fantastic! They have a large tent set up where the show takes place, but surrounding the tent they have many little tents and areas set up for drinks and relaxation.

In 2009, there was an Australian themed "Come Walkabout" section. They had a real Kangaroo to take a picture with. She was very sweet, until I made the mistake of petting her on the head. Apparently they hate that. She got angry and tried to hit me! I apologized and we made up.

# SUSAN LUCCI: THE QUEEN OF DAYTIME

Erica Kane--a successful, seductive vixen won over the hearts of millions not only in the fictional town of Pine Valley, but throughout America. Since 1970, this fiery character was known for her drama and high maintenance lifestyle on the soap opera *All My Children.* For decades people tuned in to watch what Erica was doing. Her character was always played by the talented and forever gorgeous, Susan Lucci.

Over the years, I spent a good deal of time with Susan at various *Daytime Emmy Award* shows, as well as a few other events. Many of these experiences were personal highlights in my career. I was shocked to discover what she was like when the cameras were turned off.

## *Daytime Emmy Awards* 1999 - New York City

I was thrilled to be escorting at the show when Susan Lucci won her first Daytime Emmy award after nineteen years of being nominated. Hoping she would win, I ran out into the house for a seat in the audience just when the Best Actress category was about to be announced. I had been escorting Lynn Herring who was then starring in the soap *Port Charles,* but she was in her seat already watching the show. If Susan was to win, I wanted to experience it with everyone else, and see her live on that glorious stage.

**Susan Lucci and I at the ABC Party after she won her first Emmy!**

When her name was called as the winner the entire place blew up with applause and excitement. Sitting there in the middle of it all felt like a cross between a Super Bowl victory and Times Square on New Year's Eve! I have never experienced an audience more excited than at that very moment. People had tears in their eyes and others were jumping for joy. I stood and applauded, but felt a little in shock, realizing it finally happened and I was there to witness it live. I was so happy and wanted to congratulate her in person. But backstage was a mob scene and the show was nearly ending. I figured it would be easier for me to speak with her at the ABC Network after party I was sure she would attend. Besides, she didn't know me at this point and this was a moment she should share with family and friends.

Once I finished up my escorting duties, I left the venue and decided to walk to the party located only a few blocks away. The moment I stepped outside I could see it was a crazy scene. People shouted. Horns honked. Even police and fireman ran their sirens in honor of Susan's win. Reporters lined up for their 11:00 PM news story. It seemed as if everyone on the street supported Susan. I practically skipped my way to the party.

By the time I arrived, Susan was still wide eyed and proudly clutching her trophy. She was probably a bit overwhelmed with everyone's support. I asked her for a picture and she gladly obliged. Below is that picture. It is one of my favorite of all time. Way to go Susan!

## *Daytime Emmy Awards* 2008 - Hollywood, CA

At this point in time, I had been working shows for almost ten years and had the luxury of knowing enough people that I could get my parents tickets to watch the show. They were thrilled to fly in for a visit with me and Oliver, but also the added bonus to get an inside glimpse of what I have been doing all these years as a celebrity escort. They heard plenty of stories and seen me on television dozens of times. But this was the first time they would actual get to see a show in person. My mom had been an *All My Children* fan for over thirty years. My dad would always roll his eyes whenever she and I discussed the latest character storyline twist. Both of my parents however, were excited at the possibility of meeting the legendary Susan Lucci, who I was to escort once again. After all these years of watching, my mother had only briefly met her that one time at the QVC taping many years prior.

I had met and escorted Susan a few times already, and it had always been a pleasure. Susan is so super nice that I first thought she was fake or being very "Hollywood." How could a woman this famous and in the spotlight for so many years actually be this kind and appreciative? During my first time escorting her, I quickly realized she was genuine and a woman with a heart of gold. I knew introducing her to my parents would be easy and not disappointing.

I arranged for my parents to meet me in the lobby of the Renaissance Hotel located in the heart of Hollywood. At the time, when Susan and her husband Helmut would be meeting me to leave for our red carpet arrival. The hotel was just a few hundred yards from the Hollywood Walk of Fame and where the red carpet was laid out. That year the show was taking place at the Kodak Theatre, the same place as the *Academy Awards*.

I had first met Helmut years back. At first he came across as stoic. But after speaking with him the first time, I soon realized he was a sweet man who was extremely supportive of his wife. Not only that, but on numerous occasions over the years of escorting her, I could see that even after forty plus years of being married, they were still madly in love with each other. Something I had hoped to find one day.

My parents arrived on schedule and quickly became giddy on adrenaline after seeing various actors from *All My Children* and other daytime shows in the lobby. Most of the celebrities were staying at that hotel so it was a hubbub of stars. My mother nervously waited by the elevators with my dad, the *All My Children* publicist (Michael) and me, as Susan and Helmut were reportedly on their way down.

After a few anxious minutes, Susan came off the elevator looking beautiful. It always surprises me that no matter how many times I see her, EVERY TIME she takes my breath away! I was prepared to make the introductions when my mother and father beat me to it. They both introduced themselves to her and Helmut. I took a few pictures with my mother's camera when all of a sudden several photographers showed up taking pictures of their own. My mother and father both looked stunned as they were not used to the numerous flashes in their face. It was a flash frenzy. I needed to break up this moment to get Susan to the red carpet and away from the quickly developed gathering of fans. To this day I don't know which media outlets those photographers were from or what ever happened to those pictures.

Susan, Helmut, Michael and I, headed out the front doors of the hotel and into a waiting limo. We were only a short walk from the red carpet. However, that day the weather was extremely hot (almost a hundred degrees) so the less exposure to heat the better for us all. I wanted to ask if my parents could ride with us in the limo, but it was a very unprofessional request so I pointed them in the direction of the carpet and said I would see them inside. They didn't mind walking and understood I was working. However, they wound up pretty much walking along side our limo as we barely moved due to the traffic. I wanted to walk the carpet with my parents, but a good friend of mine, and fellow talent team member, said he would take care of them and give them the "celebrity walk" experience as we had previously discussed.

**My Mother, Catherine Gaida, and Susan Lucci
moments before Susan was to walk the red carpet.**

The minute we hit the carpet it was disgustingly hot. The tuxedo helped hide the sweat stains, but did nothing to keep me cool. Susan was a trooper and didn't complain a bit. Helmut noticed some friends so he walked ahead of us to speak with them. Luckily, someone from production gave us an umbrella and Michael held it while the three of us clustered under for shelter from the brutal sun. We stayed on the carpet for quite a while making sure Susan did as many interviews for eager reporters as we could before scurrying inside for the start of the show.

The show was amazing, as always, and I felt guilty I didn't have time to check in on my parents. I did see them from a distance, a few times. They appeared happy and had great seats.

Once the show ended, there was a dinner afterwards for the celebrities and VIP guests. My parents only had tickets for the show. I could only get them so far and security was tight when it came to the invite only dinner. I wanted them to have the entire experience, but what could I do? I didn't know the dinner was so selective and with no time to work my magic, they were going to be kicked out.

Without my knowledge, earlier in the evening, my mother found dinner tickets on the floor and cleverly had the forethought to pick them up. When security came over to ask them for their dinner tickets, my mother pulled out two of them. I almost fell over because she had the proper tickets and they were served dinner immediately. Crisis averted. Like mother like son! I was amazed and proud. Go mom!

Afterwards, I told my parents Susan and Helmut wanted to attend the ABC Network's after party. I wanted to make sure they got there safely with no difficulties. I explained to my parents I wished they could come as well, but I didn't have tickets for them. Instead I would meet them a few minutes after dropping off Susan and Helmut. My dad told me the evening had been an incredible experience and they would be fine with heading back to their hotel. My mother agreed, but for me it didn't feel right to say goodnight just quite yet. I told them to walk with us to the party. I probably would have no problem getting them, in as long as we are all with Susan. They agreed. The plan worked without a hitch.

My parents were amazed by the ambiance of their first Hollywood party. I explained they could get any drink they wanted from the bar and it was free. The look on my dad's face was priceless. My dad is a man who has worked hard all of his life. When he hears anything is free, he wants to know the catch. Although he seemed skeptical, my parents headed toward the bar anyway as Susan, Helmut and I merged into the center of the crowd.

After making sure Susan and Helmut were happy and with friends, my job was done. I found my parents standing off to the side watching everyone. My mom was sipping on a white wine. My dad was on his second Manhattan (his favorite drink). He was surprised the bartender not only knew how to make it, but the drinks were, in fact, free. We stayed for about an hour sipping on drinks, people watching, and eating some hors d'oeuvres. They mentioned several times they had an incredible evening before walking to their hotel just up the street. I stayed a little longer to chat with my fellow celebrity escort friends.

To this day, I am so grateful they were able to experience this world for an entire evening and to see firsthand how exciting my job truly is. For once, I think they understood why I keep escorting at shows and hanging out with those "Hollywood types." They realized not everyone in this industry falls into the stereotypes you often read and hear about.

## *Daytime Emmy Awards* 2011 - Las Vegas

More recently, I was handling talent flow for the show, but also helped by escorting Susan Lucci, once again. It took place at the Las Vegas Hilton for the second year in a row. The show itself took place in a ballroom. At the end, everyone funneled out the doors, located at the back of the house. Many of the slot machines had been moved to make a small pathway for the red carpet to the front doors of the casino. Hours earlier, this area had been the official red carpet. After the show it remained the carpet for people to exit out of, leaving up the extensions to hold back the fans.

There was also a cleared pathway that led to a set of elevators. They were quite a distance away, but it was the only route that led to the after party. As the pathway reached closer to the elevators it became increasingly narrow. Security was placed at various points to hold back fans who had not been part of the audience. However, the audience/fans/ticket holders that watched the show were mixed in with the celebrities so it quickly became very chaotic.

I led Susan and Helmut down the path while fans became wildly excited as all the favorite daytime stars flooded out of the ballroom. We had a long walk to the elevators so I tried to rush Susan along as she signed some autographs and shook many hands. The thing I discovered about Susan Lucci is that she truly LOVES her fans. Every time I have escorted her she has gone out of her way to meet them and take pictures. This night was no different. The crowd started to worm around the extensions, walking on the carpet and surrounded us and the other soap stars. She tried to greet them all and was posing in pictures one after another. This seemed like it could quickly become dangerous, so I rushed her along and told fans that we had to keep moving. Of course, many didn't think I meant those words as they continued to try to get close to her and beg for a quick photo. She was very gracious and wanted to accommodate them, but I insisted that she didn't have the time to stop any more. Usually I am very nice with this. I understand the fans' point of view, however, things were getting out of control. I needed to make sure Susan was safe. Besides, I am sure we all wanted to get to the party at this point. If she stopped to meet everyone, we would be there for hours.

**Susan Lucci: Always happy and requesting to meet the fans with her husband nearby. Class A woman all the way.**

When we reached the elevators, three hotel security officials were already positioned there for some added assistance. They had blocked off fans from this elevator bank so only people attending the party or people with rooms, requiring that elevator could enter. There were a few party guests already by the elevator doors anxiously waiting. When the elevator door opened, the people waiting filled the elevator. Just as the door was about to close, one security guard held the doors open and asked everyone to exit the elevator so that Susan, Helmut, our guests and myself would not have to wait. They clearly recognized Susan as a star and wanted to give her their version of VIP treatment.

Horrified at such a request, Susan told those people to do no such thing and she would wait for the next elevator. She thanked security, but told them it was not right. These people were waiting first. The last thing she wanted was for them to be inconvenienced for *her*. The people did exit and gave up the elevator. Susan was embarrassed and thanked them repeatedly as we entered the elevator quickly. The elevator doors closed with only us in it. We headed to the Penthouse Suite. She was now out of the public eye, so I knew the next moment would confirm what I already knew about her. After about two seconds of silence, she stated she felt bad the security guard asked them to get out for her. She hoped none of those people were in a hurry or upset about the inconvenience. Her publicist and I reassured her they were okay and that everyone knew it was security's doing, not hers.

This was one of those special, private moments where a celebrity reveals their true identity. I already knew Susan was an incredible human being, but I was still so very proud to be by her side. Most people would not have said anything or even worried about it, but she cared moments later.

Fun Fact: Every year I have escorted Susan to the *Daytime Emmys*, I noticed something interesting. Before the start of the show, while everyone is running around to get to their seats, the orchestra plays music. This is common and happens at every award show. However, no matter what song they were playing, or in the middle of, as soon as Susan and I would enter the house and walk toward her seat, they played the theme song from *All My Children*. I have never heard a song specifically played for any other celebrity (while the cameras were not rolling) at the *Daytime Emmys* or, in fact, at ANY award show I have ever worked! Yet, it occurred year after year. A chill ran down my spine every time I walked in with Susan because I knew what was about to happen. When it did, it was as if we are transported into Erica Kane's town of Pine Valley. It is always really cool to hear it and makes me smile just to think about how special and loved Susan Lucci is. I guess she truly is the Queen of Daytime Television!

One final note on Susan: When my mother was in the hospital and battling cancer a second time, she created a video message wishing her a speedy recovery and had ABC's SoapNet send over lots of *All My Children* merchandise. This was before Susan had even met her at the *Daytime Emmys*. She knew it was my mother and that she was a fan.

If you still wonder if Susan Lucci is similar to Erica Kane, I would say they are in terms of all of Erica's good qualities. But Erica's bad qualities seem to be nonexistent in Susan Lucci.

# AFTER THE AWARDS...PARTIES

The celebrations after the award show host says goodnight, are often the most exciting and entertaining part of the entire evening. Stars who have sat quietly for two or more hours, some winning, others forcing smiles when they hear another name called, are eager to move on to the next part of the evening and make their grand appearance at the velvet roped after party. Hollywood has mastered the art of glamorous excess. I for one say, why not? If you have the money, live it up!

I have heard some people complain there are *too* many award shows, *too* many parties and Hollywood is some sort of self-congratulatory ego factory. After all of my experiences, both as a mere mortal and being part of the "in crowd," my opinion is that, people don't celebrate enough! Hollywood has gotten it right. Why not honor each other's hard work and loyalty no matter what job you have? Instead of attacking the people who do celebrate, shouldn't we all step up and celebrate the victories and accomplishments in life more often? Wouldn't the world be better if we all got awards for our hard work and huge accomplishments? Personally, I think if awards were handed out more often and if there were more parties at every work place, everyone would be happier and more productive.

With that attitude in mind, I take advantage of every after party celebration. After a long day of being by the side of a famous person, I am exhausted. Imagine, all day long people grabbing at you, battling to get close to the person you are standing next to. Your guard is always up and you constantly look all around for the nearest exit to make a clean getaway if the scene becomes too unpleasant. It takes a great deal of energy to handle all the needs for the production of the event and the celebrity. So by the time the show is over, while tired, I am always up for the exclusive after parties to celebrate yet another successful event where I maneuvered an A-lister through madness. Besides, where else am I going to be able to rub elbows and table hop with the best that Tinseltown has to offer?

**Beautiful ice sculpture at an after party held at the Las Vegas Hilton**

At this point in the evening, fans are more hyped up than ever. They have been waiting anywhere security will allow hoping to get a close-up glimpse of someone famous. Celebrities and their escorts try to get backstage as quickly as possible to be shielded by the overzealous fans who are now released from their seats. Gracious stars will often sign autographs, pose for photos, and give some lucky individuals bragging rights for their Facebook page. Producers and those who wish they were, pack the already crowded hallways of the venue eager to get thirty seconds to establish some sort of connection with the talent, or at least grab a quick photo for their "friend," "spouse," or "kid." There is additional chaos of hundreds of audience members leaving while tired crew workers try to clean up as quickly as possible so they can get home to their families--or to the parties.

This is the part of the evening I call "post-show purgatory." All I can think about is after party heaven! My back aches, my shoes are even tighter, and the sweat still brews underneath my undershirt. Sexy! Unfortunately, during this time there is a great deal of standing around waiting for my talent to leave. I usually spend this time standing off to the side trying to gauge whether my talent is ready to go or actually interested in the conversation they are having. A simple glance of their eyes would be my cue to pull them away. Business is business though, and celebrities need to network as much as the rest of us. Impatient managers and nagging publicists try to push the star to the party, but I feel my job is to allow them this time to attend to whatever affairs they desire. The drinks will just have to wait a few minutes longer.

When the celebrities are ready to go, one of two things usually occur: We head over to the after party, greeted by uniformed wait staff and walk right in, treated like royalty OR the celebrity I escorted for the evening has decided she's had enough and would like their limo to take them home. A few of them even end up at a drive through window grabbing the ease and comfort of their favorite burger. This second option is definitely not my preferred choice because many times that means I am on my own--without tickets to the party. You would think that for all my efforts helping the Kings and Queens of Hollywood by making sure the shows runs flawless would earn us, celebrity escorts, a ticket from the production staff, but we are usually overlooked.

The food at every party is always incredible. I tend to
have a sweet tooth and go straight to the desserts first.

After all these years my name has been added to many lists and sometimes I do get tickets. However, this was not always the case. This had never stopped me though because I ALWAYS get into the after party, one way or another. Over the years, I have perfected my covert missions into party crashing and would love to share them with you. First let me share some stories about the parties I've crashed. Then I'll spill the beans in the next several chapters.

## *The Essence Awards* 1999 - New York City

The *Essence Awards* was one of my very first shows as an escort. Hot on the radio and club scene, at the time, was "Nobody's Supposed to be Here," sung by the extremely talented Deborah Cox. When I arrived early that morning to meet her for the first time, I was taken aback by her innocence. She was adorably shy and polite, even confiding in me that she used to sing in the closet as a child because she didn't want anyone to hear her! On the stage that night, she was no longer the shy little girl in her closet. She was sexy and confident with a voice that reached far into the back of the theatre. Hearing her sing actually caused a chill to go down my spine.

Bolstered by her well-received performance, she was eager to get to the after party, with me at her side, as I had been much of the day. Since this was still all very new to me, I stuck to her side, only leaving to grab her a drink. I was in shock by the exquisite party with free flowing booze, flawless wait staff, and a food spread that could feed Africa. Looking back, I was very clingy, because I wanted to do a really good job. She seemed to enjoy my extra attention, maybe even liked my company, because when she and her entourage of two announced they would be leaving and heading to another party being hosted at her hotel, she invited me to join them.

I had already been overwhelmed by the environment I was in and fearful I might push my luck if I lingered with them too long, I politely declined. I told them I'd stay at this party and relax a bit on my own. I also wanted to allow this amazing evening to penetrate my brain so I could remember every detail vividly. We exchanged our good nights. I was left with the day swirling around in my head, mixing well with the champagne I'd been consuming. I grabbed another glass of bubbly from the overstocked bar and walked over to a railing that overlooked some of New York City's most amazing buildings. Lost in thought and having a hell of a good time, I didn't see at first the older Hispanic man sauntering over to me with a bit of a leer in his eye. He said he had noticed me the moment I walked in. It became very obvious he was interested in more than just casual party conversation. He was pretty direct in his approach; in fact, very clear, and very *graphic* in what he wanted to do to me (since this is a family-friendly book, I won't repeat the colorful language and imagery he used). After I politely declined his X-rated offer, he told me his name. When his name meant nothing to me, he was surprised. He proceeded to tell me he was a member of the group The Village People. Hoping he would not burst out in song, I told him I knew of the group and appreciated his offer, but I wanted to be alone. He handed me his business card just in case I changed my mind and headed out to a limo parked below. To this day, every time I hear Y-M-C-A, I think of our conversation and laugh.

Even after hearing his colorful language and learning a few new terms, I still felt on top of the world and decided to take a walk home. It is funny how people and music can affect you so much. I was rapidly approaching my cramped one bedroom apartment when I heard music from a club that was still open. I decided to grab one more drink and savor the moments of the evening. After about a minute at the club, and in the process of ordering my first and only drink, Deborah Cox's song "Nobody's Supposed to be Here" began to play. I looked around as if someone was playing a practical joke on me, but of course there was no one there I knew. I wanted to tell someone about how ironic this was, but I figured no one there would care. So I just grinned and enjoyed the song quietly to myself while sipping on a very strong vodka and Diet 7UP.

My experience with Deborah was only the beginning of how quickly I could form a bond with celebrities. In fact, one of the reasons I escort to this day is my ability to be real with them and make a connection. Most of the time they love the extra attention I give them and they include me as part of their entourage for the entire evening. In Las Vegas, this was certainly the case.

## *VH1 Divas Duets* 2003 - Las Vegas

It was a very hot day in Las Vegas at the MGM Grand when I found out I was assigned to escort Queen Latifah to the *VH1 Divas Duets* show. I had been an escort at a few other *VH1 Divas* shows already so I knew what to expect. The only difference this time was this *Divas* show was in Sin City. When I had first found out I would be escorting Queen Latifah, I was disappointed. At this point in my career I was given or requested by top celebrities and at the time, Queen Latifah was just a rap artist in my eyes. I was not into rap at all. I knew she was on a TV show, but I knew nothing about it, so she was not on my radar. In addition, I had worked with a former colleague of hers that was a *very*

210

difficult and bitter woman. I assumed Queen would be the same way. I quickly told production I wanted someone else to escort, but they said they really needed the strongest escort on her because she was the host of the show. They wanted everything to be perfect for her. I didn't want to make production think I was difficult, so I reluctantly accepted the assignment.

Much to my great surprise, Queen Latifah (also known by her friends as Dana) was the happiest, most fun lady I think I have ever escorted. She was extremely radiant and her joking attitude was passed straight down through to the rest of her staff. I met her and her assistant LB (a tall, thin black woman who I later found out knows how to really balance work with having fun) in the lobby. Together, along with the hotel bellman, we went up to her room at the MGM Grand. The moment the door swung open, everyone, including Queen, was blown away with how large and elegant the room was. She even asked the bellmen if this entire suite was just for her. To our surprise he said yes. This two-floor suite had huge windows that overlooked the Las Vegas strip and must have had four or five large rooms in it. There was even a private elevator in the suite that reached the second floor. Each room was filled with lavish furniture and was even more grand then the room featured in the movie *The Hangover.* To this day, it is the best hotel suite I have ever seen in person or featured on any television show or movie.

Since Queen Latifah was the host of the show, the entire day was filled with rehearsal and some segments that needed to be pre-taped. It was sometime in the early afternoon when we went to the top of the parking garage to shoot Queen riding a motorcycle. Her grand entrance for the start of the show was her arriving by motorcycle; so for logistical reasons this needed to be taped and edited early. Although it was hot outside, we had a great time shooting and it was fun to see how these segments are put together later. We continued rehearsals on stage and then all of us got dressed and ready for the show.

During the *Divas* show, LB and I worked hard to make sure Queen had everything she needed and we were on top of timing and wardrobe changes. The evening was a lot of work, but fun. I felt very connected to them both.

We were in the final thirty minutes of the show when LB broke out some vodka from the fridge and asked if I wanted to start celebrating. Tempted, I refused and told her I was still working. She said I had done an incredible job and we were almost finished so it was all-good with her. I told her I didn't want to be drinking on the job because I take escorting very seriously, but if she happened to pour some into my red bull can then I would be happy to drink it. LB poured some in and we did a toast to a successful, long day. We joked about my low tolerance, so I was cautious to not drink too much. I did feel a little guilty because I never drank while working. I am very old school when it comes to being professional. This time though I figured if they didn't care, then I didn't either. I think sometimes I am the only one who worries about this sort of thing.

The show was a huge success. With our work finished, it was time to make our way to the after party, which was located very close, just outside by the pool. I walked Queen and her small entourage through a special hallway I discovered earlier. I knew by taking this route there would be less people around and we could arrive without being stopped a dozen times. Everyone else took the "normal" route and there was a pile up of people delaying those celebrities and creating a more stressful walk.

When we reached the entrance we were greeted with smiles and walked right in. The party was, *amazing*. Tables of food everywhere, open bars sprinkled throughout and a dessert table that would send a diabetic into shock by just looking at it. Queen and LB headed to a table to relax while I bolted directly to the closest bar. She was safely in the party, happy and I was proud of yet another successful show. I was officially finished with my duties so now I could *officially* drink. After getting a margarita with no salt from the bar, I decided to wander around. At every party I attend, I love to first scope out the crowd to see if I knew anyone. Then I find the best food.

Although it was cooling off outside, the evening was still very warm, so I downed the sweet tasting margarita. My mind became foggy from the lack of water consumed and the high concentration of alcohol that rushed through my blood stream. I still felt I was in control and no one would notice I was a little drunk. I knew I didn't have to drive later and it was free booze so I felt comfortable consuming several drinks that evening.

After bumping into a few friends and catching up, I noticed on the beautifully lit pool deck there was a great deal of people now mingling. The party was now in full swing and this was my time to network. I headed over to the crowd and maneuvered my way around in search of more familiar faces. As I circled the pool trying to stay focused on my hunt, I felt too close to the edge of the water. I stumbled backwards to avoid taking an unwanted and embarrassing dip. With my jerking back motion, I knocked into someone else standing behind me and close to the edge. *Oh man*, I thought, *I could have fallen into the pool.* Quickly realizing I bumped into someone, I turned to apologize and realized the woman I had bumped only was not pushed in only by pure luck. When I turned to see whom I knocked, I almost fainted right into the water--it was Whitney Houston!

*Oh My God! I almost knocked Whitney Houston into the pool.* That would have ended my career for sure! Thankfully no one made a big deal about it. I apologized profusely, but Whitney just continued her conversation to the people she was with. At least she wasn't yelling at me! The shock of the realization of what almost happened quickly sobered me up. I stopped drinking immediately. Still shaken by what just occurred, I stood next to a table full of munchies. I stuffed my face, partially using it as an excuse to sober up, but mostly because I love desserts. It was my reason to consume as much as I wanted without feeling guilty. Every little dessert and cheesy appetizer tasted as if it was the best morsel I ever consumed. A few friends found me devouring everything on the table and started to do the same as I told them the story of what had just happened. We decided to play it safe and people watch as we discussed our plans for the next day.

As we talked I watched several guests leave, taking gift bags as the exited. I was wondering what goodies were in them when something interesting caught my eye. Remember the reality show star Omarosa? She was the tough talking businesswoman on Donald Trump's show *The Apprentice* who eventually was fired. Well, she had been the big "star" that year and everyone loved to hate her. As I watched the table I noticed she would grab a gift bag and put it on the ground a few feet away. She went back a minute later to different person handing out the bags and grabbed another gift bag. She did this four times! Maybe she was taking advantage of her fifteen seconds of fame, or possibly she was getting them for friends. But regardless, it seemed to me that she was up to something.

Finally, one of the gift bag attendances noticed her repeated bag collecting routine and told her politely she needed to leave because she had already gotten her gift bag. Omarosa put up a little resistance, but quickly grabbed her bags and left. I am not sure if she was drunk or what the issue actually was. Of course, I made sure I grabbed mine on the way out after drooling over the thoughts of trying to get two bags myself.

Escorting Queen Latifah taught me the valuable lesson to always keep an open mind. In addition to being a hundred percent wrong about her and having a fun filled day, a few days later I got a call to audition for a lead role in her next film! Something she (or at the very least LB) recommended me for. That she thought of me and suggested me for a role in her movie, when I was just an escort at *one* event with her, was really touching.

## A Few Days After the Show...

I was back in LA when I received a call from LB who said I would be getting a call from a casting director about Queen's next film *Taxi*. It must have only been a minute or two later when a casting assistant called asking for my address and telling me I was to audition the following morning. She explained that a courier would be at my apartment in two to three hours with the script with all the information. Sure enough, someone came to my door with a large manila envelope around 3:00 in the afternoon. I excitedly tore open the envelope to find a script, four pages of sides (the lines you are to read for the audition) and specific instructions including a map of the FOX lot. *Wow, I am auditioning at FOX.* I had a lot of friends who went for auditions at little production offices or casting spaces throughout the city, but at an actual studio was practically unheard of unless you were already a name. I had never had the opportunity to be on that lot so that only made everything all the more exciting.

I looked over the sides and noticed I was to be playing Queen's boss. *Wait. That must be wrong. How am I supposed to play her boss?* This seemed liked wrong casting as I pictured a fifty-year-old fat guy as a boss of a taxi driver. Regardless, this was my shot. I highlighted my lines on the four pages and read them obsessively over and over again. I made notes on the page on how I was supposed to act, but felt very nervous and knew I could not memorize all these lines in less than twenty-four hours. I decided I needed to read the script so I would understand the full story and maybe be able to play the character better than someone who has not taken the time to read it. I was certainly not used to reading scripts so one hundred and eight pages seemed daunting. I wished it had been shorter.

I climbed into bed next to Oliver and started to read. I read and read and read, but I must have been reading at a snail's pace because before I knew it, it was well into the evening. I became very upset and nervous because I still didn't know my lines. My thoughts were also torn in two different directions because I wanted to get sleep so I would look good for the audition--I also thought I should go to the gym to help me look my best. I choose the gym for a forty-five minute overhaul and

216

then went straight to bed. I told myself that in the morning I would have to spend another hour going over the lines before leaving.

The next morning seemed to come too soon as my alarm pulled me out of sleep jolting me awake. I jumped out of bed in a slight panic and went immediately to the kitchen to eat a little breakfast while reading through my lines. The role required me to be in a suit so I put my one and only black suit on and headed to the studio. Of course it took longer than I expected with Los Angeles traffic. Thankfully I had given myself extra time to get there so I arrived with fifteen minutes to spare. I pulled up to the large metal gates and showed my driver's license to the guards. They directed me on where to park and told me where building twelve was. Thankfully there was plenty of parking.

I was a nervous wreck and sweating in my cheap suit. I headed into the building and searched for the room number. When I reached the door I stood outside for a second, wiped my brow with a handkerchief I managed to remember to stash in my suit jacket pocket, and opened the door. Several men were sitting down on folding chairs that lined two of the walls, and there was a table straight ahead for check-in. I signed my name and sat in one of the three empty chairs all the way at the end. There were five guys already waiting to be auditioned. They all seemed young like me so I hoped the description of the boss was wrong and they wanted someone young.

As I looked around to scope out my competition, I noticed some of the faces looked familiar. In fact, they all looked like people I had seen on TV before. *Oh great. How am I supposed to compete?* I had this terrible feeling of panic. I wanted to leave, but I had managed to get this audition and spent all night studying for this role so I had to follow through with it. I wished the role just required one line or maybe two. That I know I could have nailed. I would have been happy to be the guy in the film who's a waiter or doorman, not a big role with lots of lines. Then with the next film I could work my way up. When I had more confidence.

At the time I had basically zero acting experience, except if you count the few extra roles I had on several TV shows and movies. As I tried to focus and give myself a dose of self-confidence, it came to me. The one guy sitting across from me, I had seen before. He was on the TV show *The Facts of Life*. I had watched that show every week when growing up and he was the kid that starred in the last few seasons, Mackenzie Astin.

My knees literally knocked, as I knew these people were far more experienced then I. Waiting for my name to be called was torture. It seemed as if hours passed, I headed into the room with a big forced smile on my face. The casting people were very nice and had me try the lines three times. I thought I would get away with doing it just once, but it was good they asked me to do it several times because I could feel myself become better with each attempt.

When I left the audition room I knew I would never hear from them again--and didn't. It was clear to me, at the time, I was not ready and not right for the role. The role did go to someone named Christian Kane. I was just happy I went out of my comfort zone and did something I never thought I would. It felt like a huge success on many levels from reading an entire script in one night, to working on the lines, to having the guts to audition and make it through to being on the FOX lot for the first time. This was a great experience that caused me to grow and I have to thank Queen Latifah and her assistant LB. To this day, when I do see LB at an event, she calls me her red bull buddy, which I find very endearing. As far as Queen, to me, she will always be the Queen of Cool.

## *VH1 Divas: An Honors Concert for the Save the Music Foundation* 2002 - Las Vegas

A dear friend of mine, and veteran of many award shows, had the pleasure of escorting one of the Kings of Las Vegas, Mr. Wayne Newton. After my friend and I completed our duties that night and, the frenzy began once again to get them to the after party. This time it wasn't just a walk to a banquet hall, but a drive across town to the Palms Hotel. Cyndi Lauper, who I escorted all evening, had left already, so I was trying to figure out how I could get into this party.

It was at this point my fellow escort and Mr. Newton emerged from the back of the MGM Grand. Wayne it seemed, had driven one of his many Rolls-Royces to the venue and would be driving himself home--electing not to attend the party and therefore not needing his limo. As the true gentleman he is, he offered us his after party tickets AND a limo that production assigned to him for the night. After thanking Mr. Newton, we giddily hopped into the twelve foot long black stretched car, settled into the leather seats and made our way to the Palm for an amazing night in Vegas. This was the kind of star quality treatment I could get used to. It goes to show you how nice even legends can be.

## *Spike TV Video Game Awards* 2003 - Las Vegas

What happens in Vegas stays in Vegas? I think not. My experience escorting one of the hottest women in the world should be shared, especially when everywhere we walked tripped over each other just to get a glimpse. It was comical to watch, yet at the same time, absolutely astonishing to see the power one blonde woman's beauty can have. Many people think they know her, *all of her*, but they really don't. The controversial and gorgeous Pamela Anderson has a lot more to her than what has been in the media. Although it was only one day, my experience escorting Pam made me change my opinion about who I believe she really is.

Before escorting Pamela Anderson, I was a fan and not because of her huge boobs and flawless face. She's really a character and enjoyable to watch in her many roles on television. I also loved her sense of humor and comedic timing, especially on her under publicized television show *VIP*. I did, however, think she was playing herself and just another hot actress in Hollywood who leaked a sex tape. I was wrong.

There are three things about Pam that surprised me. (I hope Pamela is not upset about revealing my thoughts, but these are things that caused me to love her even more.)

First, I thought she was an excellent mother! Who would have thought this former Playboy Model would actually be a great mother? From the moment I met her, she was very protective of her two adorable sons. She made sure they stayed close to her, away from the cameras and chaos of an award show. When it came to be her time on stage or she had to have detailed conversations, her mother jumped in and took over bringing them back to the hotel room. Pamela never wanted them exposed to the press. And when many actresses would be focused solely on themselves, she appeared to be thinking about them all the time. I could tell nothing meant more to her then her children.

**I was a lucky guy to be escorting Pamela Anderson in Vegas!**

Second, I believe she is very intelligent and a savvy businesswoman. It was interesting to see Pamela transform physically and emotionally right in front of me. At one point in the green room, we were having a casual conversation about a bunch of things. Her responses and opinions were very interesting and thought provoking.

221

Then, all of a sudden, I saw her physically straighten herself up. She shifted the way she spoke. I wondered what happened until I someone with a video camera taping us. She transformed into this ditzy, seductive woman. It was almost like she was a different person. I believe she is a better actress than many give her credit for. The fact she has been able to work consistently and is one of the most well-known names in the world, says a great deal. I think many women should admire what she has pulled off (and I don't mean her clothes).

Third, Pamela is very sweet. I always tend to think the popular, hot girls are snobbish and bitchy. Pamela was far from that. Her generous heart seemed to be as big as her breasts! She was very happy to meet her fans and even signed autographs on the red carpet. She treated everyone with the utmost respect and appreciated anyone who helped with anything. Behind that stunning face is a stunning person and for that reason I feel ashamed to have first misjudged her.

Later that evening, I was lucky enough to be invited to party with Pamela. Together, with a small group of people, we quickly left the venue and headed through the casino to a small bar called Tabu. As we walked, the crowds grew larger and larger. They began to follow us. It became so large, I felt obligated to help her security keep fans and gawkers at a distance. When we arrived at Tabu there was no reservation, but management quickly found a table for the ten of us, which included one of her good friends and fellow actor, David Spade. Champagne corks flew and two hours later we all seemed to become best friends. I am not one hundred percent sure who paid for the tab, but I believe Pamela did.

From there, our group walked to another casino bar, meeting up with Anna Nicole Smith (who was sadly wasted or incapacitated in some way). All of us had another round of drinks and hung out for a bit more. By this point, as much as I didn't want the night to end, I was beat and needed to get some sleep before I passed out on one of those beauty's voluptuous breasts. That would be embarrassing! I said my goodnights and headed to bed.

What I took away from this experience is to never judge a book by its cover. We have all heard this expression, but it's true. Whether created by Pamela or by the media, there is a perception of her that is wrong. She is not this ditzy bad girl people believe her to be (Pam if I'm blowing your cover, I am sorry). It was a pleasure to see this sweet, genuine side. Because of that I love Pamela Anderson even more than ever.

## *Happy Days: 30th Anniversary Reunion* 2004 - Los Angeles

Over the years celebrity escorting has afforded me a variety of incredible experiences. In 2004 it transported me, for the first time, into the innocent world of a 1970's sitcom. *Happy Days* was a television show I grew up watching. The prospect of spending time with Mr. and Mrs. Cunningham, Richie, Joanie, Potsie, Ralph Malph, and the rest of the gang was a real thrill. The show lasted for ten years on ABC and presented an ideal look at family life in the 1950s-1960s. This classic television show's thirty-year reunion aired as a two-hour event, but was shot over the course of two days. I was thrilled to be a part of this show's legacy and spent both days with one of America's favorite television families. My cousin Jim was visiting from New Jersey so I brought him with me to give him the ultimate Hollywood experience.

**Pretty cool cake Mrs. C had on her kitchen table**

The first day of shooting took place on a softball field at the pristine campus of Pepperdine University in Malibu, CA. It was a hot Saturday in September. I was asked to escort Marion Ross for the entire day. (Marion Ross played the matriarch of the family, Mrs. Cunningham--also known fondly as "Mrs. C".) The cast was playing the game for charity as they had during all those years while taping the show. It felt as if I was attending my own family reunion, except none of them knew who *I* was--truthfully I only knew their characters, not them. It was a very intimate day with no fans, a small crew and just about the entire cast in attendance. They seemed excited to see each other. I could feel the love and bond they shared even after all of these years.

**Marion Ross, Me and Tom Bosley**

Probably the biggest star from the show, Henry Winkler, who played Arthur Fonzarelli "Fonzie" or "The Fonz," was the first to arrive. The Fonz went beyond just being a TV character; he became a legend, an icon and made his way into the lexicon of American's everywhere. He was, and still is, the epidemic of cool. His original motorcycle from the show was parked for all to see. Watching him touch it for the first time after all these years was an amazing experience. He was really moved, as if seeing an old friend and even teared up after hopping on it. Henry seemed like an excited child all day long as he carried his *own* camcorder around to make sure he captured all the rare behind-the-scenes moments. The chances of an actor making it on a hit show are astronomical, but to be on a show that actually touched millions of lives is magical. Only a small group of people can say that. I felt emotional, myself, observing their trips down memory lane.

Jim was originally going to hang out with me and just observe, but when the catcher didn't show up for practice, Gary Marshall recruited him. Gary wanted to warm up with his daughter Penny Marshal, so Jim became the catcher. He later escorted Penny for part of the day, but ended up escorting Pat Morita who played Arnold, the owner of the cast hang out, the Drive-In. Pat had been the last to arrive and was very late, but Jim was great with getting him up to speed and very attentive to his needs.

After a day of softball and rehashing old memories in the hot sun, everyone was exhausted, yet Marion Ross came over to thank me for all my hard work. It was an easy gig; I just stayed with her and made sure she drank plenty of water. There was not much required of the escorts, since it was low key and everyone had been friends with each other already. Throughout the day Marion was very sweet, sometimes checking in with me to see if I was enjoying myself. After a big hug she handed me a piece of paper. Scribbled on it was her home address and a hand drawn map of how to get there. She told me I should come to the after party she was hosting and there was no need for me to change my clothes. It was in an informal gathering and that I should just show up in about an hour for some dinner and drinks. I was speechless. She was just like her character Ms. Cunningham. Honestly, I felt like I was in a new episode of the show. Here I am a complete outsider who escorted her for the day and she was willing to not only open her heart to me, but her private home as well. *She really is Mrs. C,* I thought.

Of course I was going to go. How could I pass that up? I told my cousin Jim and he just about fell over. It was like telling a five year old he was going to have dinner with Mickey Mouse. I thought his head was going to burst with excitement. All day long he had been whispering that this day was the best day of his life. Now he had an entire evening to look forward to.

Ignoring Marion's advice of coming as we were, we raced to my home and quickly cleaned up. We were both sweaty and dirty from working ten hours outside, and although we were not dressing up, we wanted to put on some fresh clothing. I was very paranoid about losing the map so I kept an eye on it as if it were the Holy Grail. I was afraid that if I somehow lost it, we'd lose out on this once in a lifetime experience.

When we arrived at her house in Woodland Hills, CA, a valet attendant took my car from us. *Very fancy,* I thought, as I had never experienced a valet at a home before. My best friend, and fellow escort Michael, had arrived at the same time. Together, we headed straight to the back yard where everyone was gathered. It was a surreal experience. My eyes couldn't soak in enough. Just about the entire cast of this iconic show was there, and so was I. The large, well-manicured lawn surrounded a deep in ground pool. Servers walked around, keeping everyone satisfied. The yard even had a putting green off to the side! Toward one side of the house, there was a large rectangular sand pit that peaked my curiosity. My cousin later explained to me it was a bocce ball court. He wanted to play, but was too shy to start a game with his childhood heroes. I told him to hold off because no one was playing. I had no idea what bocce ball was and didn't want to annoy anyone.

It appeared no other crew was there. It felt like just a cast party where everyone had years of memories and experiences with each other. Amazingly, not one of them was rude or asked why we were there or who we were. They were extremely nice and cordial, treating each one of us as if we had been a part of their lives forever. I felt more at ease when Marion noticed we had arrived and gave me a hug, once again, welcoming us. We were given a brief tour. She had lots of food, drink and a *Happy Days* cake prominently displayed on the kitchen table. It looked amazing. Since most of the party was in the beautiful backyard, we grabbed some beer and gathered under the moon lit sky.

After some chit-chat, my cousin, Jim, noticed Ron Howard arrived. He desperately wanted to speak with him. He pulled out a camera, which made me afraid he might embarrass us. Before I knew it Jim, walked over to Ron and introduced himself. Michael and I quickly followed. We spoke to Ron for several minutes with Jim leading the conversation. I tried not to be a fan or annoying because this was their reunion. We were lucky enough to just be there. However, Jim seemed to win him over because it didn't take long before Ron took a picture with Jim and they started to talk about *The Last of the Mohicans*. They continued to talk for quite a while. I was impressed with my cousin's ability to rub elbows with one of the best directors/producers alive!

My cousin wound up playing bocce ball with Marion and her family until late in the evening. Michael and I watched as Marion's family competitively kicked my cousin's butt back to New Jersey. We stayed so late playing and laughing, the valet had already left and my keys were sitting on her kitchen table.

**My cousin, Jim Raffaele, and his idol Ron Howard**

That entire day was a magical experience. Some fans would beg, borrow, and steal to just get a glimpse of their favorite TV characters-- but almost never does a fan get more than that. And there I was, hanging out late into the night with the entire cast of *Happy Days*. It's one of those moments that make me smile every time I think of it. If that was still not enough, we had to meet everyone the very next day for the second and final day of taping on a studio stage where we were a part of many more enjoyable memories.

# ENRIQUE IGLESIAS
# HELPED ME CRASH A PARTY

Many of my after party experiences have allowed quality and fun time with celebrities. But sometimes the talent I work with requests to attend the party alone or prefers to go home, leaving me stranded. It's certainly not their obligation to make sure of my happiness, nor do they have to allow me to continue to escort them to the party. Usually my role is complete once the show is over and my talent leaves safely. Many celebrities also assume that I have tickets with or without them, so they never worry about my ability to attend.

One example of this was the *GQ Men of the Year Awards* in 2000. The talent I was escorting left immediately after the show. I was certain, though, I'd have no trouble getting into this post party on my own, honoring GQ's celebrated men from entertainment, fashion, and sports. But, it was a party that almost didn't happen for me. This was when I learned just how generous a famous person could be.

### *GQ Men of the Year Awards* 2000 - New York City

I had the pleasure of meeting Enrique Iglesias one day prior to the show while escorting him during rehearsals. Most often an escort stays with their talent for both days, however, I had already been booked to another celebrity for the actual show. Enrique's escort was not available for rehearsals so I jumped in to help her out.

When I meet Enrique for the first time, I knew very little about him except for three facts; he was a singer, he was Latin, and he was a very good-looking man. When we were first introduced he was wearing a crocheted hat, street clothes, and had the clearest complexion of anyone I've ever met. I'd never seen another man so perfect looking. He was a man that all men wanted to look like and all women would want to sleep with. I became very nervous, as I do with all attractive people. What's up with that anyway? Does someone who is beautiful have special powers or something?

He shook my hand immediately as we exchanged introductions. I actually reminded him of a friend he had living in Los Angeles. At the time, I was still living in New York City and had never even been to Los Angeles. I thought it was exciting to have a possible look-a-like living there. The fact that he was nice enough to start a conversation right off the bat put me at ease. During our interactions, I realized Enrique was very laid back and probably one of the nicest guys I'd ever met. Rehearsals flew by and soon enough he left, leaving me a bit sad I was not his escort for the show.

The awards were fun as always. Actors such as Benjamin Bratt, Pierce Brosnan, Russell Crowe, Matthew Broderick, Michael J. Fox, Sarah Jessica Parker, Jennifer Connelly, and Julia Roberts were all in attendance. Dennis Miller was the host and even though the show was not live, it went by very quickly. The after party was all the buzz, as it was taking place at the Four Seasons Hotel on Fifty-Seventh street.

It was a cool, brisk autumn evening when three other escorts and I left the Beacon Theatre full of excitement and ready to party. We walked the fifteen or so blocks to the hotel hoping to arrive early enough to talk our way into the official GQ party. Heck we worked it, why wouldn't we get in? Apparently, we were too late. We were stopped at the corner, about a half a block from the hotel by security. I could hear the boom-boom-boom of the dance music taunting me as we were being denied access. Hell, we couldn't even get close to the actual entrance. This was the first after party I had been to where they actually put up velvet ropes and closed the ENTIRE sidewalk to pedestrians. It was a bigger party than I had anticipated, which meant it would be harder for us to get inside.

None of us had party passes, but we *did* have our All Access show passes hanging from our necks that we flashed the guard. This allowed us to get on the street and closer to the velvet rope entrance. But that was about it. There was another checkpoint before the actual check-in table and a beefy security guard basically snickered at our All Access, for it certainly didn't apply to what was behind him. After haggling with him, it became embarrassing. He was not going to budge. People with party passes breezed by while giving us smirks and disappointing glances. I felt as if I had been pulled over on a busy highway by a police officer. People kept passing by pleased they had not been stopped, but curious to glance and see what was going on.

One of my fellow escort friends argued with security that the All Access pass meant ALL ACCESS. The guard angered because of his tone and did one of those macho walks over to intimidate him. As he turned his back to engage in this minor confrontation, I scurried past the now unguarded sidewalk and onto the red carpet that paved the way into the party. I could see the light! It was a good distance to the check-in table at the front door, but the closer I got, the more excited I was. I didn't dare look back. I tried to continue my stride to the door, but was stopped by a tall, skinny male security guard who seemed to come out of nowhere. He uttered those disgusting six words: "Do you have a party pass?" Again, I showed my All Access badge and told him I had worked the event handling the celebrities. He pointed me towards the check-in table where he said I needed to see if my name was on a list. Relieved I made it past another guard, I calmly approached the elegant table where a twenty something blonde girl sat with a black marker in hand. If the movie *Legally Blonde* would have come out before this time, I would have probably thought it was Elle Woods. As soon as I stood in front of her, she looked straight into my eyes and simply said "no" before I could even utter a word. It was a little ironic the table was so beautiful and sexy, yet this woman's manners were so cold.

That two-letter word crushed my soul. I made it past three guards and now I was going to have this skinny "better than you" trust fund princess, tell me I could not get in. Determined to not give up, I insisted my name was, in fact, on the list. I learned a thing or two while in cahoots with my friend Debbie at previous less stellar parties. The classic, look at the list and steal a name off it, but this time though, the blonde was holding the list close to her chest. She was already a step ahead of me. Besides, with no Debbie and this being a solo mission, I was screwed!

Just when I got my final rejection and I was about to turn around to do the pathetic red carpet "walk of shame," I looked to my right. Who was standing next to me? Enrique Iglesias! Having been there long enough to realize I had pleaded to get in, Enrique asked me what was going on. I told him they were not letting me in with my All Access show pass. He asked me why. Before I could utter another word, the short blonde stood between the two of us, rudely interrupted and said, "He doesn't have a ticket, but Enrique let me get you in right away".

As Enrique followed her, my face burned with embarrassment. Then, all of a sudden, Enrique stopped, turned to the girl, and said something along the lines of, "I am not going to go to this party unless you let my friend in." Parties such as these want and *need* celebrities to go because it helps get them media attention.

She immediately said no problem and glowered as she waved me in. As I raced across the line, my heart dropped as I thought of my friends that were still stranded. I wanted to go in, but I couldn't leave them there literally on the street. While Enrique was already going out of his way for me, I pushed it a bit further and told him I was sorry, but I have three friends waiting at the first checkpoint and I couldn't ditch them. He said he would wait. I almost fainted. The little assistant huffed, fuming over what I am sure she considered a huge breach of protocol.

Without pause I ran down the carpet and hurriedly brought my friends to the entrance where Enrique still stood patiently. The four of us giggled as we passed the velvet ropes--like kids sneaking into an R rated movie. I thanked Enrique probably three times as he brushed it off as no big deal. Being that he already went out of his way for me, I left him alone for the night and only waved goodbye when I later saw him leave the party. It was truly amazing. He didn't need to worry about little old me, but he did, and I have never forgotten about his generosity.

We enjoyed the alcohol so much I became a little *too* buzzed. I was not the only one. On my way out of the Four Seasons I saw one of my fellow male escorts drunk and hanging on the shoulder of another male while kissing his neck. When I took a closer look I was surprised to see it was an A-List Academy Award winning actor! They walked out together very lovingly and seemingly drunk. I was stunned! This actor was certainly not out *at all*, and twelve years later he *still* isn't. Most people would be surprised to hear he is actually gay. While he has done a good job at keeping his sexuality from the public, I was shocked he was flaunting it so publicly at a party and that no one seemed to notice; or if they did, they played it cool.

As I stood there with my jaw wide open, some lady handed me a gift bag. Everyone attending the party got one. She must have thought I was leaving. The rest of my friends grabbed bags as well. We stood there discussing the recent discovery for a few minutes before stumbling into a cab. Eager like a young boy Christmas morning, I reached into the bag to see what I had gotten. The very first thing I pulled out was a cell phone! This was a gem at the time, especially since it became my first cell phone ever! It was 2000, so cell phones were still relatively new, especially to financially strapped people like me. I didn't want to pull anything else out of the bag in fear I would unknowingly drop something on the floor of the cab, being that I was pretty tipsy. Luckily, I got home safely *and* without leaving a trail of gift bag items.

Up to this point, I was naïve and thought these after parties would want celebrity escorts to attend. I thought our hard work and A-list connections would give us this little perk. Looking back, I believe it was this party experience that made me determined to go to any after party I wanted--whether I was invited or not. If I didn't have a ticket and was not with a celebrity, I still was going to get in! Being good, honest, and hardworking was not enough. I realized I would have to be smart. I would have to go into Secret Agent Gaida mode, bound and determined to get into every shindig, one way or another.

# TEN TIPS TO PARTY CRASHING

I love parties--the bigger and fancier the better. Which is why award show after parties are always amazing. Hollywood knows how to throw a party better than anyone in the world and they only want the cream of the crop to attend these events. Just because you don't have a ticket, doesn't mean you can't get in and still enjoy the spoils of the riches. In fact, out of all the years I have been escorting, I have NEVER NOT gotten into an after party I wanted to go to. Other escorts and friends are always amazed about my triumphs, especially after they have failed at those same events, but I believe I now have party crashing down to a science.

Let me share with you ten of my tips that will help you to get into any party you desire, no matter what event or where you live. You could use one or more of these per party, but if you just pick the best tip for that occasion, you will be golden. I warn you however, I am not responsible for any trouble you may find yourself in if you get caught. This is not something to take lightly. You could find yourself in a heap of trouble. Just because they have worked for me for over ten years doesn't mean you couldn't encounter a problem. Although very unlikely, I don't want to be getting a phone call from you in jail asking to be bailed out.

*If you are a security guard or doorman for parties, I ask that you skip this chapter.*

## TIP 1) Timing is Everything!

There is a huge advantage in planning the right time to get into a party. Typically, the earlier the better. Don't show up really late thinking security has slacked off and will not be checking. Really, you want to arrive with the earliest big rush of people when security is busy and so you can blend in. If you arrive too early though, you will stand out. Security will have time to consider rejecting you.

Security guards at parties are usually new and inexperienced because they usually happen only once a year. When you arrive as the first crowd does, they may not know how to handle a situation where someone doesn't have a ticket. Many times you can use that inexperience to smooth talk your way in or name drop. As the evening becomes later, security quickly learns they need to enforce the rules more strictly, hence killing your chances of getting in. Often, party crashers arrive late. The place becomes full. They get picked off and rejected easily. Once that starts to happen, your chances of getting in drop significantly.

## TIP 2) Team Up!

My favorite method is what I call the tag team. This is where you have two people check in together at a party. I recommend a member of the opposite sex for this to work the best because you can divvy up the flirting duties as you never know what sex will be holding the guest list at the door. While one of you engages the innocent prey in casual flirtatious conversation, the other peeks at the guest list on the check-in table or in the prey's hands. This may require a little work to get a good glimpse, but the payoff is always successful. The names will be upside down from where you are standing so you need to quickly find any name that has not already been checked off. When the prey, aka checker, tells your friend that his/her name is not on the list, then you chime in and suggest maybe the RSVP is listed under my name. You give the stolen (I like to think of as borrowed) name. If the checker didn't ask for an ID from the start, they will not at this point. The checker will search the list, find the name and let you both in. Easy breezy! This method has been highly effective in my experience.

If that person whose name you borrowed does show up later, they can always show their ID and prove they are who they say they are. The checker will not remember who gave what name and probably will think they checked off a wrong name previously. If there is more than one checker, they usually don't coordinate their lists. The name could be checked off when you used the name. The second could be used when the real person arrived. And no one would ever know.

## TIP 3) Divide and Conquer

Many times the key to party crashing is the same thing required of great magician--distraction! While working solo on a crash mission might seem like a better idea, having a small group is ideal. With a few people (no more than four) you can distract guards, making it easier for someone to sneak in. More than four can draw attention and there's greater chance of someone messing up the mission or changing the plan midstream. I always think a lean and mean group is preferable. Everyone must understand and agree on the plan before approaching the door. The key is to get at least one person in. Use one person as a decoy while the others sneak in. Once one person makes it inside, there are many other strategies to get the others in.

## TIP 4) Blend In

It is important to blend in. This is not your time to be special and try to start a new fashion trend. If you are going to a million dollar party wearing a bright yellow shirt from Sears, you probably will not fit in. The only way to fool people is to look like them. Rent an expensive tux or dress, put on some bling, do the hair up, wear make-up, and make yourself look like you *are* someone. Don't forget to be sure to wear what is appropriate for that specific event. Dressed like everyone else and fitting in, most people would never expect that you are trying to sneak in.

## TIP 5) Rush and Avoid All Eye Contact!

One important tip in getting past security at a party you were not invited to is to AVOID looking at any security or ticket collector in the eye. Keep your head low because once you make eye contact, they are much more likely to stop you. If you look busy, such as talking on your cell phone, many security guards tend to feel bad distracting you by interrupting your call. Walk by them as if you belong. Don't stop your stride if possible. They are only ticket takers after all, so they have no clue if you are a big shot producer on the phone. If you look them in the eyes, it is an invitation for them to speak to you. They will ask to check your ticket. Once you have eye contact you can't ignore their questions and unknowingly you might invite them to a conversation. Now you will have to try to talk your way into the party when before you could have just walked in.

## TIP 6) Don't Look Back!

If you walk past security and have not been asked for a ticket, you're on your way to an enjoyable evening. However, a rookie mistake many people make is turning around, curious to see if anyone noticed they made it past security. This makes you look guilty. If security notices this, they might try to get your attention and stop you. Look confident and keep going forward. Just don't ever look back! It will ruin your very short victory.

Even if a security guard calls to you for your ticket after you have passed them, just pretend you didn't hear (this really works well if you are on your phone). They must have been talking to someone else, surely not you! This also works because the chances of them leaving their post to catch up with you are very low, unless they have someone to cover. If they do come after you, the same result will happen as if you went back yourself, you will be thrown out. If you keep walking and pretend not to hear, you are more likely to get in.

## TIP 7) The Back Door

What door has no security and is always open? The kitchen! While shown in movies, no one ever thinks of *actually* entering through this entrance. Yet, it probably is the easiest way to get in. There are no guards and numerous people come and go all evening. The few times I've used this method have been very successful. Whether you are alone or with a partner (no more than three people total, again don't want to draw attention to yourselves), you simply walk in as if you belong there. You can even add some touches such as pretending to give your fellow conspirator a tour. Follow a waiter through the door to the party and walk right in with confidence. You will enter in the middle or back of the party. No one will be the wiser.

Confidence is key. Once you have made it deep into the kitchen, if someone asks you can just tell him you are lost looking for the restroom. Probably no one will, because the kitchen staff are too focused on their jobs. They will think you are a guest, not somebody who snuck in the back door, and wouldn't care even if you had. The only difficult part of this method can be finding the back entrance. Sometimes it is well hidden or you have to walk a bit. For that, you're on your own!

## TIP 8) Confidence/Story

If you have confidence and look like you belong, sometimes you can get in with that alone. If you look nervous or act scared, you WILL get caught. In case you are stopped, you must have a story ready. You work for XYZ, you are a producer of XYZ or something along the lines where it is plausible for you to be invited to that event. You need to be knowledgeable about the topic you mention. And don't make up crazy information or a story like, "Oh, I directed Jaws." People are not idiots. They will know you are lying. Some people are also well connected, so you're taking your chances if you say you are Bob Smith and they happen to know Bob. Instead of name-dropping, I have sometimes made up a detailed story. Once you have lots of details in that story, people will think you know more than them and let you in. Basically, if you have confidence and a good story that can't be disproved, you should be golden.

**TIP 9) Never Crack**

There are a few of my friends who can't handle the stress of sneaking into a party. If you feel like throwing up just sneaking into seeing a second movie for free, or not stopping at a stop sign when no one is around, then you should NOT try to sneak into a party. This is not for everyone. It takes a lot of courage and sometimes a little stupidity.

If you feel you have the confidence, then go for it, but do not crack. If someone stops you, don't break down and admit to what you are doing. You never know, they might have been stopping you for some other reason. Just stick with your story and play it cool. If you get turned down for good, put on a stern face, say you will be making a phone call, and then walk away. If you get thrown out or stopped once, I would suggest not trying again unless there is a different guard or entrance. No matter what, I want to remind you again, I am not responsible for any of your actions. If I were told to leave, I would do so and not challenge anyone. No party is worth drama.

**TIP 10) Always Use Your Head**

Figure out the best way you can get into the party. There is always a way in if you take the time to think about it. For example, at one party in New York City, my very good friend Debbie and I couldn't get in. We tried every trick in the book and just couldn't. We had a friend already in the party. After calling him, we found out he was leaving early, so we waited by the exit. Debbie, being the genius that she is, asked him if they collected his ticket. They had not and he handed it over to her upon his exit. (Some parties they don't collect the tickets or invites in case the guest wants to leave and return later.) She took the ticket, walked up to security and marched right in. I said my goodbyes to our friend and waited by the wall below where the party was going on above.

After about five minutes I heard Debbie call out my name. I looked up and there she was with a huge smile on her face. She shouted down the party was awesome and she dropped her purse down to me. It fell at my feet. Knowing how Debbie's mind works, I opened it up. There it was, the ticket! I snatched it out and quickly put it in my pocket.

I then shouted up as if to a stranger, "Excuse me miss, you dropped your purse!"

Debbie looked down smiling, almost laughing and said, "Oh thank you".

I threw her purse up to her. Okay, it did take three tries, but she got it. I then pulled the ticket out of my pocket and walked in the once impossible guarded entrance. Another victory for our duo!

# THE ULTIMATE PARTY CRASH

## *Primetime Emmys* Governor's Ball 2008 - Los Angeles

Getting into the Governor's Ball following the *Primetime Emmy Awards* telecast without a ticket, is like trying to get past bank tellers to count the money in their safe. In your mind, you think, "It ain't happening". There are dozens of award shows, and countless after parties, but the Governor's Balls for the *Emmys* and *Academy Awards* are the Grand Daddies of them all. They are lavish, gorgeously decorated, and unashamedly decadent in their offerings of delicious food, unending alcohol and fabulous music, often by top name musicians like Tony Bennett and Pink Martini. One year Seal even took hold of the bandstand for an impromptu performance that had the surprised crowd of cheering A-listers. No detail is overlooked. It's like prom night for the Rich and Famous and everyone in Los Angeles wishes they could attend.

After escorting on the grand red carpet and sitting through the three hour broadcast, three friends and I decided to try our luck. We were going to accomplish the Holy Grail of party crashing, the Governor's Ball. The Emmy award show had just ended. All the VIP patrons (with party passes) were ushered through the house side left into the lobby. Along the glass wall stood two large glass doors that opened to the outside of the building where a sectioned off pathway began. The trail ended at the convention hall where the party was being held. All along this wait staff, who looked handpicked from a model runway, bore silver trays of champagne to welcome guests to the party. Security was sprinkled everywhere with concentrations at key areas on the path. The whole procession to the party had something of an amusement park feel, like when you're a kid and you see the gates to Disneyland for the first time and you know you're in for a big adventure.

A Peek Inside the Governor's Ball

Certain our names had somehow been "overlooked," my friends and I joined the sea of patrons heading out the glass doors. Though, unlike them, we did not have any passes and were not on a guest list of any kind. We had already scoured the floor to see if anyone may have dropped or discarded their party passes, but found nothing. This is one of the most exclusive events in Hollywood and no one was going to lose their chance to get in.

Usually getting into an exclusive party is not too difficult because they have only one checkpoint to show your ticket. Some parties are more high tech and they actually scan the tickets like boarding pass. I figured this would probably be the case since it is the most exclusive party there is. My team reviewed my arsenal of " party crashing gimmicks," but we knew none of them would work here. We'd have to go outside the box on this one.

Like going into battle, we decided to divide and conquer. First, we paired off. The pathway grew more and more congested with guests eager to get in as we went our separate ways. I grabbed the first glass of champagne I could from this hot brunette server who went a little crazy with the amount of lipstick she wore. With the glass in one hand, I fished out my cell phone from my tuxedo pocket and held it snug against the scruff of my face pretending to talk to someone. I took a sip of the bubbly. Its originally intention was to be a prop for the mission, but I quickly came to realize I actually needed it to calm my nerves!

My heart pounded, but I kept thinking to myself that *I must get in*. We quickly approached the first check in area. The security people were shouting to make sure everyone had their tickets out for them to check. I did not slow down my stride. As I approached the security person another guest handed him his ticket. As he looked at the other person's ticket, I just walked past both with confidence. *Oh My God, they didn't even notice*, I thought. *I made it*. I kept walking and didn't look back. Remember, if you keep moving forward as if everything is normal, they will not chase you because they won't leave their post to come after you. They have dozens of other guests there who needed their tickets checked. If for some reason the security guard did come for me, that would only leave the area unguarded for my friends to get in. I don't mind be the sacrificial lamb, occasionally.

As it happened, I did not have to throw myself on a grenade for my friends. I made it past one more checkpoint, downed my champagne and was already celebrating my victory, eager to reunite with my war buddies inside. Then, horror struck me as I realized there was another checkpoint twenty feet ahead. *Wow! This sucks!* It would have been the ultimate humiliation to make it this far and then get turned away, so I plodded along. My heart beat so fast I was sure everyone around could hear it. With a quick look back I noticed my friends had made it as far as I had. They looked relaxed and cool as a cucumber. *How did they have this courage?* I really became nervous and could feel the sweat pushing out every pore of my body. I could no longer do a fake phone call, I was so nervous I knew I wouldn't pull it off. I needed to talk to someone, even if it was talking about nothing. I needed to stay calm and focused.

Needing a lifeline, I decided to phone a friend, for real this time. I punched in the number of my childhood best friend, James. I knew his would be a soothing voice and keep me from freaking out. *Please answer, please answer,* I thought as the phone rang once, twice, three times. Then James answered, thank goodness. I explained to him I was making a brave attempt to break into the Emmy's Governor's Ball and I needed someone to talk me off the ledge. James was the perfect person to call, because instead of asking me a million questions about who I was with and who else I saw famous, he proceeded with random conversation that relaxed me enough to trudge on.

During my *(real)* phone conversation, one security guard asked to see my ticket. Cradling the phone and still holding the fluted champagne glass, I gestured with my chin that it was in my coat pocket. He told me I needed to take it out for him to see. He then turned to check someone else's ticket, I kept moving, not missing a beat, still talking to James, and flowing along with the crowd. Of course I didn't look back to see if the man was coming after me or calling security. When I didn't feel a hand on my shoulder after a few seconds, I knew I was free. I could see my friends had had equal success up to this point. It made me proud, watching them bounce along, nervous as cats on the inside, but calm, cool, and collected on the outside. The four of us were like CIA operatives on a very dangerous mission. We were almost in.

We did the same maneuver past one more checkpoint. I kept thinking about how crazy that we were getting away with this. This party was like Fort Knox, and yet I was sneaking in! I felt like an evil genius. When we reached the top of the staircase where the actual entrance to the party was, I took a moment and looked back at all the people being funneled in and all the checkpoints we had to pass to get to this point. It felt as if I had just completed a marathon. For a moment, I felt a little guilty about sneaking into a party I was not invited to, especially such a huge important one as the Governor's Ball. I knew it was wrong, but I really did feel we worked so hard to make the show as glamorous and as fun as we could; we handle all of the talent logistics, problems, and drama after all. Why would they exclude us from the invite? Happily justified with my decision and full with the rush of adrenaline continuing throughout my body, I went back to focus on the party.

About to reward myself for the victory, I realized we *still*, weren't in. There were several doors open for guests to enter the party, each with an Academy representative there to inspect tickets one last time, *holy crap, another one?* Still separated, my friends and I picked a doorway, eyeing the ones with the most crushing crowds in hopes of getting lost in the shuffle. I thanked James and told him I'd better get off the phone. I took a few deep breaths. I HAD to get in now. If a person has made it this far I think they deserve to get in. Like that would work as an excuse if I got caught, "Oh you made it past our security and don't have a ticket, why go right in, we are proud and amazed you achieved such a feat, you deserve to be inside with Hollywood's finest." I'm sure that is what I would hear if I got caught…right.

I walked right up and the female ticket taker at the door immediately asked for my ticket. Each guest had to stop and show his or her ticket one by one. I fumbled around in my jacket pockets in a feeble to attempt to show her a ticket I didn't have. I gave a sheepish grin. I "knew" it was here somewhere. I felt a knot in my stomach when she told me to step aside so guests with visible tickets could go in. As she kept checking tickets, I stepped over about five extra feet. My hands were shaking at this point. I noticed my friends had made it past the party doors, still pretend chatting away on their cell phones. I was more nervous now than when I jumped out of an airplane to get over my fear of heights. (It didn't work and I just hyperventilated 14,000 feet down.) Now, I was about to hyperventilate. I had no desire to get busted, but I also didn't want to go home either, especially after coming all this way and seeing my friends were waiting for me. I took a few deep breaths and thought that Secret Agent Gaida needed to get in. *Stay calm no matter what*, I told myself. *I needed to do this.*

Mustering up one final bit of courage, I slinked away one door over just as a B-list celebrity and her entourage were coming through. I stayed close behind them, told the ticker taker I was part of the group and we all walked in. It was as simple as that, I was in! When I think back on it, I can't even remember who the celebrity was that unwittingly brought me in as part of her crew, but no matter, I had made it. *It worked!*

Half shocked and extremely relieved, I stood only a few feet in the party when my friends came over to celebrate our united victory and compare stories. It was thrilling to see everyone accomplish this silly goal. But, I felt we needed to step away from the entrance area immediately and get lost into the party crowd for us to not to be discovered as the ultimate party crashers we had become. All three friends felt I was being paranoid because we were already in, but they followed my lead. We quickly headed to the bar, grabbed four champagnes and toasted our feat.

The ball did not disappoint. Fancy tables with glistening centerpieces, ice sculptures at the bars, silver sofas perfect for cocktail conversations and impromptu pitch meetings, delectable food and desserts. I had been to many parties in my day on both coasts, but this was one of the most enjoyable, mostly because it took a hell of a lot guts and determination to get in. Every current television star seemed to be there. Most people sat down and enjoyed the dinner. We wanted to do the same. However, because we did not have tickets, we also didn't have seats or a table assigned to us. We could always find some empty seats, but it would be highly embarrassing to be in the middle of eating when the person with that seat showed up. We decided to make do, though and walk around and eat fancy little treats of decadence while making new friends.

I text a reporter friend of mine who I knew would be at the party, to see if we could meet up to say hello. He immediately responded and told me what table number he was at. After briefly telling him our adventure, he allowed us to join him at his table. He had to interview many of the winners and couldn't sit anyway. So not only did we get in, we now had seats and a catered dinner! Every morsel of food and every sip of beverage tasted its fullest. The music was classy and fun. We met some interesting and talented people all while being in the midst of numerous celebrities. We just fit right in the entire time as if we had that golden ticket.

**Revisiting those cherished doors to the Governor's Ball almost one year later.**

# PUTTING THE HAPPY BACK INTO GAY

*Rosie O'Donnell's a LESBIAN!* When the press splashed headlines about her sexual orientation all over the supermarket rags and even the nightly news, it didn't surprise me one bit. What shocked me is that reporters didn't announce it earlier! When I was escorting her at the *Daytime Emmys*, we were backstage with her then girlfriend Kelli. In plain sight, I saw them kissing. This lip locking session was a very loving moment and not something to shock people like when Madonna kissed Brittany and Christina at *MTV Video Music Awards* in 2003. Rosie's kiss only lasted a mere second or two, but when I saw everyone around behaving normal as if nothing happened, I was surprised.

"Why isn't this big news?" I wondered at the time of the kiss. Apparently, she was not hiding her identity or her feelings for another person and lots of people knew--yet no one discussed it. Reporters never covered the story and no one talked about. At the same time, rumors flew around about other stars such as Ricky Martin and Tom Cruise are gay. I stood there thinking if someone had taken a picture, it would have been worth big bucks and possibly destroyed her career. This was an era when letting the public know about being gay seemed to be a career killer in entertainment--as Ellen's coming out supposedly ruined her sitcom. And yet there was Rosie living her life for all to see without hiding.

It actually was nice to see the kiss in person and for no one to make a big deal. On the other hand it was weird, because it was so open and normal. I was not used to that and also had never seen lesbians kiss in person. I was a bit relieved they could be left alone and a witch hunt hadn't begun.

About seven months later, Rosie did come out in a bold and aggressive way. This may not have gone over well with many people, but she was out and definitely not hiding anything anymore.

As a celebrity escort, one of the top questions I get is asked is, who is gay in Hollywood? I understand this question is on many people's minds, but it's not something I would answer even when I know the truth (and trust me, there is a lot I know I'm not telling). It's a personal choice for someone to "out" themselves and sometimes a difficult one for them to make. Although it has becoming easier, there is still a lot of hate, confusion, and moral conflict in society. Whether someone is a celebrity or not the fear of being judged is present. When a career and money are involved, things tend to become even worse. I know this struggle all too well. In case you are not aware and have not realized it…I am gay.

During my early years of escorting, I kept it a dark secret because I worried it would affect my ability to get work. *Could I be gay and still escort female celebrities? Would people hire me knowing I am gay? Would I be thought of first as my sexuality and not my ability?* Questions always rattled around in my head and the topic made me nervous to even think about.

In fact, I kept being gay hidden from everyone until after I graduated from college. I knew a few gay people while attending American University and even had a boyfriend for most of my time there, but I was nervous people would think of me differently if they knew the truth. I wanted people to like me (or not) because of who I am, not because of one aspect of me. I also didn't want it to be a big deal even in a positive sense, such as someone being proud and introducing me as their gay friend. I just wanted to be *me*. Being gay is just a portion of who I am, like maybe, ten percent of the overall me.

In addition, I was prejudiced toward gay people myself! Yes, gay people can feel prejudice toward other gay people. There really weren't any gay role models out there, well at least any that were like me at the time. While growing up, the normal chatter by everyday people was gay men are creepy, weird, immoral, weak, and wore dresses. I certainly didn't think I was any of those things, nor would I want to be grouped in with people like that. So, of course I struggled with my own identity, although deep down I knew and feared the truth. I felt different than anyone the media labeled gay. So for many years I tried to ignore my desires and didn't date anyone until college. I just wanted a "normal" life with a house, a dog, a good job, lots of friends, someone to share it with, and for no one to make a big deal because that person was another man.

## My Coming Out

In 1997 I secured an apartment with two awesome straight roommates, John and Brad, who didn't care at all about my sexual orientation. Both only knew me for a brief time prior. They quickly became part of my family, like long lost brothers. They are still my dear friends. Once, I felt confident my living situation was taken care of, I mustered up the courage to tell my immediate family about my secret. I was fearful that armed with the truth, I would be tossed out and labeled as an embarrassment. It was one of the scariest things I ever had to do.

I told one of my brothers over the phone and a second brother during a chat online, because I was too scared to do it face to face. The two brothers were the test run and everything seemed to go relatively well, despite their surprise. My third brother I decided to wait and tell later because he was the oldest. I thought he would be the one who would take the news the hardest. Now that I was peeking out of the closet and it seemed that both brothers would still stay in my life, it was the time to tell my parents.

Still living in Washington, D.C. and having just graduated from college several months before, I choose a weekend to make the drive to Pennsylvania and break the news. I was scared to death to do this in person, but felt I needed to show them that respect. I also hoped if they physically saw me, they would realize that although now out, I hadn't changed into someone they didn't know. I made the decision to tell them separately, as I didn't want one person's reaction to affect the others. I also was stalling a bit to tell my father because he especially holds many Catholic and old school values, which I mostly admire and agree with, but not when it comes to sexual orientation.

I told my mother on a Saturday and my father the following day. It came as a shock to them, but luckily both handled it respectfully. I think it took a little while for the news to sink in and for both of them to FULLY accept it, but it was not the war zone I feared. In fact, there was no arguing or yelling at all! They both loved me for who I was. The sense of relief I felt was incredible. An hour after telling my mother, she actually bought me crystal candle sticks for my dining room table. Even though I am sure she and my dad had lots of emotions and thoughts to sort out, I believe that gesture meant she was reaching out (to me and whomever I choose to share the candlelight) and saying everything will be okay. She was right. I headed back to DC, but I asked my parents to break the news to my oldest brother. I was just emotionally worn out. I never asked them the specifics of what was said or his immediate response, but I know that all was well after a few weeks. My entire family behaved the same way as we always had. It was a dream come true! After years of hiding the truth, I had a new outlook on life and was able to move forward.

With this new sense of freedom, I found out my own prejudice was, in many cases, worse than other people's. I still battled this "media" image of what a gay person was supposed to look like, act like, dress like, and behave like. Although there isn't anything wrong with many of those things, it was not how I wanted to be. I just wanted to continue on as I was, not to transform into another person. I was proud of who I was and more importantly who I was becoming.

Now that I was out, I felt free to go to gay bars, yet I was scared to death going into one for the first time. You would think it would be easy for a gay person to enter a gay bar, but I had to circle around it for over a half hour before taking my first step in. Once inside, I cowered in the corner scared to death someone would grab me or I would be forced to dance as they did at the Blue Oyster Bar in the movie *Police Academy*. I survived the experience without such antics and quickly realized there are a variety of types of gay people no media had ever covered. Just like with straight people, there are many subcultures. There seemed to be something and someone for everyone. You just had to look. I could  be myself. Because of that, I have made many incredible friends. For me, homosexuality is only one part of a person. A person's personality is what makes me determine whether they are a friend or not. There are asshole gay people just like there are asshole straight people! There are also sweet, intelligent people from both groups as well.

## Charity

I was very happy with how my life was going and relieved about my good fortune, so when I was asked to volunteer my expertise at charity events, I jumped at the opportunity.

Various organizations hold events throughout the year to support certain causes. Charity events are enjoyable because celebrities *want* to be there to give their support, unlike some award shows where they are there to promote a project. While working on charity events, I get to meet many icons who don't attend award shows regularly. For example, while escorting at the *Angel Ball Benefit* in 2000, an event that raises money for cancer, I was able to see Michael Jackson and President Bill Clinton. They were both only a few feet from me at various points throughout the evening. Michael was sitting at a table for much of the evening, while Bill was walking around shaking hands and speaking with everyone. Both were heavily guarded. I was not escorting either of them so I didn't even attempt to introduce myself. When you have a President of the United States at any event, you can just imagine the security, background checks, and bomb sniffing dog action. I didn't want to do anything that could land me in trouble with the Secret Service.

Over the years, I worked many different charity events and enjoyed my experiences. So after all my good fortune with coming out, I wanted to give back a little and use my time to support gay organizations I felt were excellent causes. Two of my favorite organizations and events are The Trevor Project's *Cracked Christmas* (now called *Trevor LIVE!*) and GLAAD's annual event, *The GLAAD Media Awards*. These are solid, excellent organizations that help put out positive truthful messages about the LGBTQ (Lesbian, Gay, Bisexual, Transgender and Questioning) community. Yes, that's a mouthful!

In addition, I wanted to give my support and time back to a community that needs additional help and awareness. These events have grown in strength over the years. Both, straight and gay celebrities and guests proudly support these events, and generous sponsors, give money to keeps many valuable programs alive and running smoothly. They have positively changed lives forever.

In the last decade it has been amazing to see the celebrities who have had the courage to come out of the closet. A new generation of gay is coming forward: people who want to be themselves and are proud of it. I feel there are now actual role models such as Ellen Degeneres, Neil Patrick Harris, Ricky Martin, Anderson Cooper (only to name a few), that shine a bright light so gay people live their lives honestly, open, and inspire future generations. There had been a few role models in the past, but they did not have the platform to be as vocal and to reach into homes every across the United States, and even the world, as we now have.

I hope celebrities continue to have the courage to come forward and come out. Like it or not, celebrities are role models for children and when someone has the courage, it spreads throughout the world. Too much ignorance and self-hatred exists and although Gay Hollywood has made enormous strides, there is a lot of work to do just by being themselves. I am not asking for a big gay agenda, just for gay people to be treated equally and fairly. I have been very lucky to have found the man of my dreams who happens to share the same name as me, Kris. Even though I have been out for a while, it can still be scary to hold his hand in public or especially, to give him a kiss. When I do, it's not to make a statement or for some noble cause, it is because I love him and like any two people in love, we want to express it.

A man can dream! My fake win as I borrowed someone's statue at an after party. So awesome to hold the real thing and think about all the talented people who have received this award.

# CELEBRITY TID BITS

Trying to write this book and to make sure *you*, the reader, gets a full view of this unique world has been a difficult task. I have compiled and condensed over ten years of my celebrity-escorting world into this one book. I easily could have filled two or three books. I tried to be as straight forward as possible, while at the same time, share my true feelings and thoughts that occurred to me during these events at the time. There are many stories and interesting facts that didn't fit neatly into the chapters.  I had to gather many of them into a chapter that resembles a junk drawer of a book. It's not "junk" per say, but treasured small moments and observations that didn't need full stories. I hope you enjoy these little celebrity morsels.

## The Tip

Normally, celebrities don't tip escorts. It's probably not something people even think of. However, there has been a few times where I did receive a one and it's always unexpected. Obviously, it is a nice gesture and appreciated, especially if the day has been long and difficult. Most of the time our "tip" is attending the after parties, freebies from the gift lounge, and for me, a hug and a "thank you" goes a long way. I did want to share the experience of the first time when I was tipped.

Marg Helgenberger, then star of the top rated show *CSI*, was the celebrity I was escorting at the 2004 *Grammy Awards*. During rehearsals, we strategized how we planned to approach the red carpet. I told her to leave home earlier then she was normal because traffic is always difficult in downtown Los Angeles, especially when a big event like the *Grammys* is taking place.

On show day, I was told she anticipated leaving her home later than we had discussed; someone on her team told her she still would get there with plenty of time to. I eagerly waited for two hours on the red carpet as star after star walked passed me and still no Marg! The red carpet began to shut down and the show began when finally her limo pulled up. They had been stuck in traffic and lost, I believe so she missed all of the interviews and press. Obviously frustrated and disappointed, we made the most of the evening and enjoyed the show.

We worked well together. Off camera she was a hip mom. When the show ended and I was walked her to the limo to say goodnight, she handed me a cash tip for escorting her. She said she felt bad because she wished she had more money, but I thought she was generous enough. At that point, I'd never received any tips from celebrities. I was thrilled. I was so moved by her generosity that I used some of the money to buy her flowers and send them to the set where she was filming two days later. A year or two later, I ran into her at another show. She remembered our experience. She told me the limo company felt terrible about having her late arrival and her missed grand entrance so they gave her free service for a year! I thought it was great. She put kindness in the universe by tipping me and kindness came back to her.

## The Scariest Thing I Have Ever Encountered

There is nothing scarier to me at an award show than a star struck pack of twelve-year-old girls. I was working a show where Zac Effron was sitting in the audience quietly minding his own business. I was not escorting him, but I noticed during the first few commercial breaks one or two girls would gather up some courage and get up from their seat to say hello to him. He didn't seem to mind the attention and when the next segment of the show began, they would go back to their seats. I was busy handling other escorting tasks, but noticed this trend was worsening with more girls giving it a shot at meeting their celebrity crush.

Then, during one commercial break, a swarm of girls seemingly out of nowhere surrounded him. There had to be twenty to thirty young women. He was forced to stand as they lunged at him from every direction. With security nowhere to be found, I ran in to save the day. When I reached him, I didn't know what to do! I was already on the outer circle of these girls so it's not like I could be a block between him and them.

The venue had plenty of security, but they were all by the doors and outside trying to make sure unauthorized people were not getting in. These were authorized ticket holders. It quickly became a scene. There seemed to be very little I could do because you can't touch people or push them away without the threat of being sued. Many other crewmembers stood shocked and unable to initiate a plan of their own.

I did the only thing I could think of: yell at them and threaten they would be forced to leave if they didn't return to their seats immediately. Another talent team member, sounding like a drill sergeant, joined me in my efforts. Together we managed to verbally scare some of the girls away. A small opening formed. I was able to reach Zac and stood in front of him with my arms out holding the wall of girls. One by one, they returned to their seats, just in time for the next act of the show to begin.

The next commercial break two security guards stood by him to prevent and future attempts. I have never seen anything like that in the house of a show ever. Zac did look incredible that evening, but come on!

## Stuck Up and Snuck Out

While at the *26th Daytime Emmys* in 1999, I had the privilege of escorting Lynn Herring (yes this was the same year and show that Susan Lucci won her Emmy). Lynn had roles on both *General Hospital* and *Port Charles* and her husband was a soap star as well. Right from the start we hit it off.

Back then, the *Daytime Emmys* had a dinner before the actual televised award show so Lynn and I were just starting our evening together. We finished the red carpet and the next step was to bring her and her husband to the pre-dinner located at the same venue, Madison Square Garden. We were heading up the stairs when security stopped us and asked to see our credentials. They said the dinner was for talent only. I had to stay downstairs and wait while they ate. Lynn told security I was her escort. I should be allowed up there. Security told her it was not possible. The crew is supposed to stay downstairs and I was considered crew. Lynn once again said I was her escort. She wanted me to join them for dinner. He refused my admittance once again. Then

Lynn said the completely unexpected (I never have had a celebrity go to bat for me like this ever!) She stated she wanted to speak with Dick Clark the Executive Producer of the show. She was a presenter on this show and if I couldn't join them for dinner she was going to leave. They would have to find another presenter. The security person radioed something on the walkie and then after a few seconds reported I could join them. *Wow, that was awesome!* I thought, happy she stood up for me. As we walked up the steps she said she thought it was ridiculous I would be working this event and they wouldn't allow me to eat with them.

When we entered the large dining room, we walked around for a bit. It seemed as if everyone from daytime television was starting to eat. Lynn pulled me aside, saying she felt it was a little stuffy and asked if there is somewhere else close-by where we could grab a quick bite. I knew of a little bar across the street that probably had burgers and finger food. She said, "Perfect." Luckily I had done my obsessive walk throughs and remembered an exit door in the stairwell that lead us right out to the street by the bar.

Together the three of us carefully vanished from the crowd and minutes later we were having dinner across the street. The bar was almost empty, but a table of fans noticed and asked to take pictures. They even said they thought I was a soap star and took pictures with me as well! If you were one of those people, I would love to see the picture! They paid the bill and we snuck back into the theatre in time for the show. No one was the wiser.

## Woody

One cute story I left out when mentioning my experience with Julia Roberts in San Francisco includes her son Henry. He must have been about two years old at the time, in Julia's dressing room before the show began. Tom Hanks and Rita Wilson were in the dressing room next door to hers. I mostly hung out in the hallway to not crowd them. Julia came out to talk to me while Tom came out of his dressing room to talk with Julia. They must have only spoken for about a minute and Tom went back into his dressing room.

Seconds later, Henry came running out of Julia's dressing room and into Tom's shouting, "Woody, Woody!" It took me a second to realize what happened. Tom played the voice of Woody in the *Toy Story* movie franchise. Henry, hearing that same voice, thought Woody was there. It was so cute and everyone laughed. Children of celebrities want to meet their favorite stars, even if he is an animated cowboy!

## Hangover After Party

I finished working at the *Golden Globes* when I noticed Bradley Cooper quickly engulfed by adoring women in the lobby of the Beverly Hills Hotel. The *Globes* took place in the ballroom. All guests and celebrities exited the same doorway into the lobby that branches off in many directions--mostly all leading to different parties. I was heading to one of the parties when I noticed this chaos. I asked Bradley if he needed some help, as he and his assistant seemed to not expect this onslaught of attention. He quickly responded yes. Thankfully he was heading to the same party as I was. Since I have attended the InStyle's after party for many years, I knew the exact route to take. We quickly maneuvered our way through the fans.

**Bradley Cooper and I Attending the InStyle Party**

Once safely at the party, we went our separate ways, but while standing in line for the buffet, I noticed Mike Tyson behind me. Being a huge fan of *The Hangover*, I was thrilled to see two cast members in a matter of minutes. It quickly seemed the entire cast was there so I pulled out my camera and had a friend of mine take a few pictures. I thought it was pretty cool to be drinking with the cast of the biggest drinking/hangover movie ever. The next day, I added some pictures to Facebook saying I was Hung-over with the *Hangover* guys. Nerdy I know, but it was fun.

**Mike Tyson and I met in the buffet line. Super nice guy but I would not want to fight him for the last dinner roll.**

## Additional Tid Bits

Darryl Hannah asked someone to hold her flight so she could ride the roller coaster on top of the New York, New York casino.

While escorting Jacyln Smith at the 2005 *TV Land Awards*, her daughter told me a unique thing. If you close your eyes and listen to Sally Field speak, she sounds just like Jacyln Smith! Or, I should say they sound like each other. I have tried and it works. Her daughter said she would hear Sally on television as a kid and think her mom was on.

While escorting Angelina Jolie down the red carpet of the *Golden Globes* in 2012, she refused to be separated from Brad Pitt when being rushed off the carpet and into the live show. I thought it was very sweet that she stood her ground and said she was not going in without Brad, since numerous people tried to get her in. Brad was doing an interview and did not want to cut it short, although there were numerous attempts by production staff. They both did make it into the show on time and everything was fine.

Thoroughly enjoyed escorting Angelina Jolie
down the red carpet of the *2012 Golden Globes.*

I was escorting an event in New York in 1999 when I went to the bar in the lobby to grab myself a soda. The show was already started and things were running on time. I was tired and had a few minutes so I had a seat at the bar next to an African-American gentleman. We started to talk and he was really cool. After a few minutes, two fellow escorts called me away from the bar to talk to me. I thought maybe my talent needed me so I told him it was great meeting him and walked away. My escort buddies giddily asked me if I knew who he was. I shrugged my shoulders. They said I was talking to Lenny Kravitz. This was a clear example of how people just want to be treated as people. He probably knew I had no idea he was a famous singer and enjoyed that we just spoke person to person. I took that lesson with me and tried to speak with all of my celebrity talent from that day forward just as people and not stars.

I was sad for Reese Witherspoon after she won for Best Actress at the *11th Annual Critic's Choice Awards* in 2006. I was her escort for the evening and I was happy she won. However, her security told me she had a stalker and everyone was on high alert. At one point before the show they thought they saw that person up a hill outside of the venue. Security communicated very little to me, which made me a bit on edge not knowing enough details. Shortly after her win, she exited a side entrance we had the car pull up to. It was just a shame the joy of her victory had to be clouded by some creep.

Celebrities have family, too. When you met them and see that they have a "normal" life, it quickly humanizes them. It's like seeing your teacher in high school on a date or at the movies. Wow, you have a life outside of class! It's actually refreshing when you see everything all works for them.

## The Lists

Everybody seems to enjoy lists. I have included a few below I think you may find interesting. This information was gathered from what I have witnessed behind-the-scenes, and is nothing more than my opinion. Each category is broken down and the celebrity names selected are not listed in any particular order. One of my requirements when choosing the people was that I had to have escorted them at least once. The decision made was based on my thoughts from only that one experience.

## My Top Five Couples in Love

I have seen many celebrities start a relationship that fails, for whatever reason, just as in non-celebrity relationships do. There are also relationships that seem to stay together more for appearance sake than the two people actually being in love. This is a list of the couples I think seem most in love. Real Love! I find their commitment and love for each other very inspiring.

1) Steven Spielberg and Kate Capshaw
2) Susan Lucci and Helmut Huber
3) Tom Hanks and Rita Wilson
4) LeAnn Rimes and Eddie Cibrian
5) Jennifer Aniston and Justin Theroux

## My Top 10 Nicest Celebrities

These celebrities went above and beyond being kind to me. It was difficult for me to narrow down to just ten, but they are the nicest of the nice.

1) Sandra Bullock
2) Hugh Hefner
3) Queen Latifah
4) Enrique Iglesias
5) Ricky Martin
6) Donny Osmond
7) Alicia Minshew
8) Rosie O'Donnell
9) Julia Roberts
10) Cameron Mathison

## My Top 5 Hottest Looking Women

Sometimes people look great on camera, but just okay or bad in person. These women looked better in person then I expected, and actually took my breath away when first meeting them!

1) Megan Fox
2) Sharon Stone
3) Taylor Swift
4) Susan Lucci
5) Jenny McCarthy

## My Top 3 Hottest Looking Men

The triple threats...Hot, Nice and Sexy

1) Enrique Iglesias
2) Adam Levine
3) Ricky Martin

## My Top 5 Most Fun Shows to Work

These shows are fun for many reasons. What they all have in common is the talent booked for each of them is always laid back and happy to be there. I believe having a happy crew is important because it translates on camera and is a better show to watch at home because of it.

1) Daytime Emmys
2) Golden Globes
3) TV Land Awards
4) American Music Awards
5) GQ Men of the Year Awards

# THE END OF THE RED CARPET

I have the most amazing job in the world where I have been able to learn many important life lessons. Over the years I encountered incredible people and experienced events only celebrities and the rich were thought to have enjoyed. I have rubbed elbows with some of the most famous stars, attended the biggest award shows in history, and shared great conversations with people from all walks of life on this thrilling journey. Event after event, I have been given all access to experience this world fully. I am extremely gratified to have been able to share many of my thoughts and experiences with you.

Over time and with each experience, I have changed. The star struck boy who never thought it was possible to meet a celebrity has spent over a decade surrounded by them. Worlds of possibility opened up as limiting beliefs and soul-destroying thoughts were shattered.

Now, for me, Hollywood seems to be a bipolar city between the rich and the poor. It is as if there is no middle class. Many people are striving to be someone or something they are not. People leave their family and friends from all across the globe to chase a dream. It appears everyone is striving to live a life style that isn't always what it seems. To us dreamers, obtaining our goal is very important, yet we tend to forget something more significant--we already have everything we needed all along! Wasn't that the lesson of the film *The Wizard of OZ*? We have the love from family and friends, the traditions in our own lives that create great joy, and the people who support us through the good and the bad. Most importantly, we have ourselves. We need to remember that when we search for validation and try to fill a void in our lives. I believe human beings are capable of just about anything we put our heart and mind to.

The television and the film industry is an awesome field with so many great privileges. But I think from time to time, everyone in this business (whether a big star or a struggling assistant) gets sucked into this world and forgets about the magic that drove us there in the first place. Most people enter this world because they have been emotionally touched in some way by television, film, and/or music. Now, they want to touch others that way. It's the only medium where you can create a human connection on a massive scale. In a way, I find that celebrities are emotional healer. They provide an escape from our lives in the form of entertainment. We get inspiration from celebrities. We live our lives vicariously through them. It's always been an honor for me to take care of someone who has touched my life and millions of others.

The dark side of the entertainment industry I have found is that most people have to uproot their lives and travel many miles to pursue their dream. Without family and friends, we are not living a dream, but bouncing through a nightmare. The stakes are high, but most people don't realize it because they are so focused on their dream. I left family, friends, and a comfortable hometown to come pursue my dream. Was it all worth it? Most times I think yes, but at other times, I wonder. I have missed out on so many wonderful things, such as seeing my nieces and nephews grow up and spending more quality time with my parents and grandmothers. This is time that can never be recovered. On the other hand, I learned a great deal about myself and the limiting beliefs we all shackle ourselves to. For most of us, our lack of faith in ourselves can be our worst enemy.

A few of the reasons I wrote this book are to show you a world you didn't know existed. I wanted to prove there's another side of the glitz and glam. I looked to highlight people are not perfect including, celebrities; I wish to inspire you to go for your dreams, but do so without having blinders on. I know firsthand how difficult the world in general is, and how much of a struggle it can be to pay the bills. I have struggled myself, but we can never lose hope of our dreams. You might not accomplish everything you set out for, but one of my favorite sayings is, "shoot for the stars, but land on the moon."

Many people wonder how all of my experiences have changed my thoughts on award shows. I love them even more now! I used to sit on my couch and wish I could be there and felt very distant from what I was watching. I previously thought these stars were spoiled, entitled people, but once I got to know them, I realized underneath the make-up and those fancy dresses they are no different than the rest of us. They might be rich, famous and beautiful, but they are all still flawed, insecure and have feelings just like the rest of us. They are people who work hard to make their dreams a reality. Knowing that, I actually find celebrities inspirational, now more than ever.

All of these thoughts are from a boy who grew up outside of Philly and made his American Dream come true. I hope you were able to get a glimpse on how much work it requires to make everything so magical. I also hope when you are at home and trying to be perfect, you remember no one is perfect and to give yourself a break. I have no idea what the future holds, but I will remember these experiences and believe in myself no matter what goals, dreams or challenges lie ahead.

I would love to hear from you and if you have any personal experiences meeting a celebrity you would like to share.

Please go to my website www.ArmCandyBook.com
Tweet me at EscortGaida,
Email me at escotgaida@gmail.com
Or Facebook Celebrity Escort Chris Gaida.

Until then keep dreaming!

Christopher Gaida

# THE ESCORT LIST

Here is a sampling of the celebrities that I have escorted, as well as the accompanying show. Shows without a name besides them means I either assisted a number of celebrities whether as an escort or in another talent team role. When a celebrity is listed, that means she or he was my focus for the entire day.

**Angelina Jolie**–*Golden Globes*–2012

*Trevor Live*–2012

*GLAAD Media Awards*–2012

*MovieGuide Awards*–2012

**Charlie Sheen**–*Primetime Emmys*–2011

**Jennifer Aniston**–*American Cinematheque Tribute*–2011

**Enrique Iglesias**–*American Music Awards*–2011

Trevor Live–2011

**Giuliana Rancic**–*UCLA Visionary Ball*–2011

**Jill Scott**–*UNCF/BET An Evening of Stars*–2011

**Susan Lucci**–*Daytime Emmys*–2011

**Rose McGowan**–*Turner Classic Movie Film Festival Premiere*–2011

*GLAAD Media Awards*–2011

**Natalie Portman**–*Independent Spirit Awards*–2011

**LeAnne Rimes**–*Grammys*–2011

**Sandra Bullock**–*Golden Globes*–2011

*People's Choice Awards*–2011

*Annie Awards*–2011

*Trevor Live*–2010

*Republic Pictures 75th Anniversary Celebration*–2010

**Fergie**–*Dick Clark's New Year's Rockin Eve*–2010

**Ricky Martin**–*Home for the Holidays*–2010

**Jenny McCarthy**–*American Music Awards*–2010

**Vanessa Williams**–*Creative Arts Emmy* –2010

**Betty White**–*Teen Choice Awards*–2010

*Spike TV Video Game Awards*–2010

*The Grammy Awards*–2010

*Golden Globes*–2010

*MTV Video Music Awards*–2010

*MTV Movie Awards*–2010

*Producer's Guild Awards*–2010

**Mariah Carey**–*Independent Spirit Awards*–2010

**Hugh Hefner**–*TCM Classic Film Festival*–2010

**Taylor Swift**–*Academy of Country Music Awards*–2010

**Taylor Swift**–*Brooks and Dunn Special*–2010

**Susan Lucci**–*Daytime Emmy* –2010

*Annie Awards*–2010

*Primetime Emmys*–2009

*Golden Globes*–2009

*Producer's Guild Awards*–2009

**Kate Hudson**–*American Music Awards*–2009

**Mary Kate Olsen**–*Independent Spirit Awards*–2009

*Daytime Emmys*–2009

**Keith Richards**–*Scream Awards*–2009

Don Rickles–*TV Land Awards*–2009

Sean Astin–*Chabad Telethon*–2009

*Hollywood Christmas Parade*–2009

*Cracked Christmas*–2009

*Produced By Conference*–2009

*80th Annual Academy Awards*–Oscar's Red Carpet–2008

*Primetime Emmys*–2008

Paris Hilton–*American Music Awards*–2008

Eva Longoria Parker–*Alma Award*–2008

Julia Roberts–*The World of Nick Adams: Painted Turtles Benefit*–2008

Annalynne McCord–*You Gotta Have Heart Benefit*–2008

Sir Anthony Hopkins–*Scream Awards*–2008

Steven Spielberg–*Home for the Holidays*–2008

*American Music Awards*–2008

*Academy of Country Music Awards*–2008

*MTV Video Music Awards*–2008

*MTV Movie Awards*–2008

Susan Lucci–*Daytime Emmys*–2008

*Producer's Guild Awards*–2008

*Cracked Christmas*–2008

Ozzy Osbourne–*Scream Awards*–2007

*American Music Awards*–2007

Paula Abdul–*Family TV Awards*–2007

Salma Hayek–*NCLR ALMA Awards*–2007

Jessica Alba–*7th Annual Taurus World Stunt Awards*–2007

Paris Hilton–*Extreme Sports Awards*–2007

Alyssa Milano–*Unicef Benefit*–2007

**Sharon Stone**–*Independent Spirit Awards*–2007

**Alicia Minshew**–*Daytime Emmys*–2007

**Sheryl Crow**–*A Home for the Holidays*–2007

**Vanessa Williams & Louis Gosset Jr.**–*NAACP Awards*–2007

**Kirstie Alley**–*TV Land Awards*–2007

*Frosted Pink Awards/Benefit*–2007

*Cracked Christmas*–2007

**Megan Fox**–*Teen Choice*–2007

**Brett Ratner**–*Producer's Guild Awards*–2007

*The 78th Annual Academy Awards*–2006

**Reese Witherspoon**–*Critic's Choice Awards*–2006

**Donny Osmond**–*TV Land Awards*–2006

**Kristin Davis**–*Cracked Christmas*–2006

*Family TV Awards*–2006

**Terrence Howard**–*NAACP Image Awards*–2006

*Spike TV Video Game Awards*–2006

**Rosario Dawson**–*Scream Awards*–2006

*Teen Choice Awards*–2006

*Alma Awards*–2006

**Cameron Mathison**–*Daytime Emmys*–2006

*Hollywood Bowl Hall of Fame*–2006

**Lisa Kudrow**–*Cracked Christmas*–2005

**Jacyln Smith**–*TV Land Awards*–2005

**Constance Marie**–*Family Television Awards*–2005

**Carmen Electra**–*Spike TV Video Game Awards*–2005

*A Home for the Holidays*–2005

**Marion Ross**–*Happy Days Reunion*–2004

Marg Helgenberger–*Grammy Awards*–2004

Courtney Love & Whitney Houston–*World Music Awards*–2004

Lynda Carter–*TV Land Awards*–2004

Jessica Simpson–*Pepsi Smash*–2004

Christina Aguilera–*City of Hope Spirit of Life Tour*–2004

*Fulfillment Fund*–2004

*ESPY Awards*–2004

*Latin Billboard Awards*–2004

*MTV Movie Awards*–2004

Pamela Anderson–*Spike TV Video Game Awards*–2003

Queen Latifah–*VH1 Divas Duets*–2003

Brendan Frasier–*Fulfillment Fund*–2003

Queer Eye for the Straight Guys–*MTV Video Music Awards*–2003

Aisha Tyler–*Big in '03*–2003

*BET Awards*–2003

*Chabad Telethon*–2003

Maroon 5–*Pepsi Smash*–2003

*William Holden Wildlife Foundation Benefit*–2003

Nicholas Cage–*MTV Movie Awards*–2002

Cyndi Lauper–*VH1 Divas Las Vegas*–2002

*Big in '02*–2002

*Thea Awards Gala*–2002

Rosie O'Donnell–*Daytime Emmys*–2001

*Come Together: A Night for John Lennon*–2001

*Tony Awards*–2001

*Essence Awards*–2001

Enrique Iglesias/Susan Sarandon–*GQ Men of the Year*–2000

Susan Sarandon–*VH1 Men Strike Back*–2000

Donna Summer–*VH1 Divas Live: A Tribute to Diana Ross*–2000

*MTV Video Music Awards*–2000

*Angel Ball*–2000

*VH1/Vogue Fashion Awards*–2000

Susan Lucci–*Tony Awards*–2000

Tom Hanks–*GQ Men of the Year Awards*–1999

Sharon Stone–*VH1 Vogue Fashion*–1999

Lynn Herring–*Daytime Emmys*–1999

N'Sync–*Celine Dion Special*–1999

Deborah Cox–*Essence Awards*–1999

98 Degrees–*Radio City Music Hall Re-Opening*–1999

Jewel–*Net Aid*–1999

Garth Brooks–*Sports Illustrated 20th Century Awards*–1999

Ana Gasteyer–*VH1 Divas Live*–1999

Mathew Broderick–*Tony Awards*–1999

*Rockefeller Center Christmas Tree Lighting*–1999

Backstreet Boys–*MTV Video Music Awards*–1999

*MTV Movie Awards*–1999

# CHRISTOPHER GAIDA
# ACKNOWLEDGMENTS

There are so many people to thank who have touched my life and have helped me get to the place where I am today. If I thanked everyone, that would be a book in itself. Here are just a few of the many very important people in my life who have emotionally supported me, helped make this book possible and/or have helped with my escorting career, which has now spanned for over fourteen years!

Special thanks to GOD for making me who I am, giving me an incredible family and providing me the abilities I needed to go after my dreams.

My parents. Dad and Mom, I love you more than you could imagine and thank you for always loving me. Even when you didn't understand or agree with some of my decisions, you have always been there and it means the world to me. You are not only great parents, but also outstanding people. I feel so blessed every day to be your son.

My entire family: Nana Gaida, Nana Heim, Doug, Tim, Eric, Karen, Jenn, Brittany, Kyle, Sean, Cameron, Dylan, Megan, Aunts, Uncles, Cousins and Grand Fathers.

Kris Brown for loving me and allowing me to love you. Celebrity escorting has made one of my dreams come true and you have made another. Thank you for proving the love and romance depicted in films, television, and in my imagination can be real and even more incredible. Thank you for making each day, whether it is a good or bad one, an opportunity to love you even deeper.

For the people who REALLY made this book possible: Michael Aloisi, Dana Newman, Dan Farrands, Tommy Hutson, Ami Manning and Tammi Leader Fuller. Without you, these experiences would have just remained as my memories.

My closest friends in life who have been there both for joy, tears, and everything in between: James Grunden, Staci Crawford and Mike Easterling.

My dog Oliver who I loved as a son and who always made my day a good day, no matter what happened. Thanks for the many adventures and always showing me the power of love. RIP baby!

Debbie Vazquez for being a great friend and partner on many of our escorting adventures.

Some other close friends who have helped me along the way: Michael Stern, Jason Palmer, Jonathan Contreras, Norman Dostal, Dianne de Las Casas, Kathryn Coulibaly, Brenda Kaminsky Leikala, Tim Stiefel, William Brown, Kimberly Lee and of course my fellow celebrity escorts.

My parents' friends acted like an extended family and role model for me while growing up. You have made a bigger influence on me than you could imagine.

Hatboro-Horsham High School and American University for giving me the best education possible, and the excellent teachers who pushed me to dream bigger.

Some of those from the talent teams that have provided me such great opportunities include: Angela O'Brien, Jeff Gershon, Caprise Arreola, Todd Britton, Dana Kenerson, Harriet Mauro and Danette Herman.

A few of the many Executive Producers that create such incredible award shows: Dick Clark, John Cossette, Ken Ehrlich, Michael Levitt, Gilbert Cates, Carol Donovan, Tom Florio, Glenn Weiss, Bob Bain, Scott Mauro, David Firschner, Don Mischer, and David McKenzie.

The great staff and crew who put in credibly long hours and hard work to create these glamorous award shows, and are normally not recognized.

To all the Celebrities who have dedicating their lives to entertaining. Thank you for the roller coaster of emotions and helping to create worlds and characters that I not only have used as an escape, but also have learned from. I also can't forget their spouses and life partners who have to put up with it all.

Last, but certainly not least...

A SPECIAL thanks to all the negative people who inspired me by telling me no, I was not good enough and what I believed I was capable of doing was not possible. Your negativity and lack of support has pushed me forward everyday so I could have an opportunity to prove you wrong.

There are many people who helped me along the way in my life and career whom I need to thank. I mentioned many of them in the book, but there are some really special people whom I want to point out directly to thank for affecting my life and career in such amazing ways.

# ABOUT AUTHOR
# MICHAEL ALOISI

Michael Aloisi, known to most as AuthorMike, is the author of horror movie legend, Kane Hodder's biography, *Unmasked* and its companion book, *The Killer & I*. The latter of which is the basis of a new reality show staring both Kane and Mike. Currently, Mike is working with another horror legend, Tom Savini on his biography.

Mike is also a celebrity blogger on FEARnet and Fangoria where he tells of his experiences with Tom Savini and Kane Hodder.

Mike's other writing include the novels *Fifty Handfuls* and *Mr. Bluestick*, the short story collection, *White Ash*, and *Tales From A Mortician*, written under his pen name, Michael Gore. With his MFA in Creative Writing and background in filmmaking, Mike has written several acclaimed short films and a dozen live action children's shows that have played around the world.

Visit www.AuthorMike.com to learn much more about his life, read his blog and to learn about his classes, lectures and future projects.

CPSIA information can be obtained at www.ICGtesting.com
Printed in the USA
LVOW082013240113

317127LV00012B/1122/P